Birmingham Repertory Theatre Company
presents

Paddy Irishman, Paddy Englishman, Paddy...?

By Declan Croghan

First Performance at The Door,
Birmingham Repertory Theatre
on Thu 4 February 1999

SUPPORTED BY
THE NATIONAL LOTTERY
THROUGH
THE ARTS COUNCIL
OF ENGLAND

 **Birmingham City Council** WEST MIDLANDS ARTS

Providing Theatre for Birmingham

Paddy Irishman, Paddy Englishman and Paddy...?

By Declan Croghan

Thu 4 Feb - Sat 20 Feb

'What we have to do now is to focus our minds on how we are going to get ourselves out of this situation'.

Kevin and Anto are mates. They're getting by; earning a few spondoolicks, cooking enormous fry ups, avoiding the bad pint and trying desperately to understand women.

But last night a good turn turned bad, and now they've stumbled into something much bigger than both of them. The situation is exploding out of all control and their Irish past is about to come crashing in on their London lives.

Declan Croghan's hilarious black comedy looks at freedom and prejudice, heroism and cowardice and asks to whom we owe our true allegiances.

Director: Anthony Clark
Designer: Patrick Connellan
Lighting: Tim Mitchell

After Dark: Wed 17 Feb (after the perf)

Trips

By Sarah Woods

Thu 25 Feb - Sat 20 Mar

'Have you ever wondered why you find a four and a half foot tall yellow cat more comforting than your own friends?'

What happens when you lose your focus in this dazzling new land of opportunity? Nik, John, Hayley, Dan and Glen are off on a night out; drugs, clubs and the fantastic twenty four hour garage. But tonight things are not quite going to plan.

Searching for love, excitement and one infallible business idea they are all about to encounter more than they ever thought possible. And what has Princess Anne got to do with it all?.

Sarah Woods' bold, funny and technologically astonishing new play combines live performance with video to explore where we are now, and where we are all heading.

Director: Jeremy Raison
Designer: Kit Surrey

After Dark: 17 Mar (after the perf)

Nightbus

By Peter Cann

Wed 24 Mar - Sat 3 Apr

'I'm not the kind of person things happen to.'

Meet Donna. She's a tour guide on one of those open-topped Birmingham Tour buses and she knows her city. The city of 1001 trades, of the Rotunda and Spaghetti Junction: the city with more parks than Paris, more miles of canal than Venice and less fun than Dudley, or so it seems. But Donna doesn't care. Hers

is a safe life, governed by electronic organisers, regular hours and familiar routes and routines.

But tonight, fate takes a hand in launching Donna into a bus-ride into weird and unfamiliar territory: into the twilight world below the flyovers: one of backstreet cosmetic surgeons and genetic engineers, of phoney traffic wardens, hotel receptionists, escaped chimpanzees, terrifying swimming instructors and crazy bargemen - all out to steal Donna's heart.

Using original, live music, five inventive performers will be

brought together in this action packed comic journey for all the family - beyond the outer margins of the city we know - or think we know.

NIGHTBUS is the first of this year's Rep Community Tours funded by the Sir Barry Jackson Trust

Director: Phil Tinline
Designer: Jens Cole

After Dark: Wed 31 Mar (after the performance)

Feb 99 - June 99

'The largest and potentially most important space outside London dedicated exclusively to new work'
The Guardian Guide

Tickets: £9.00
Concs: £7.00
Standby: £5.00
(limited availability)
Mad to Miss Mondays:
£2.99, Under 26's

Produced in association with Soho Theatre Company

Perpetua

By Fraser Grace

Thu 15 Apr - Sat 8 May

'When a person feels betrayed by the law they trust in, they start to feel there is no way to do good 'cept by forcing themselves to do bad'

Are some lives worth more than others? The town of Pensacola, Florida is about to be set alight by the fiercest of battles. A struggle that pits the law of God against the law of the land, and the right to life against the right to choose.

On one side of the city stands May Lake abortion clinic, on the other the headquarters of the pro-life extremists Operation Freedom. At the centre of both organizations is a woman with a personal crusade. As the battle rages and the stakes get higher the two women are drawn closer, with potentially murderous consequences.

Fraser Grace's gripping new play challenges our deepest moral beliefs.

Director: Jonathan Lloyd
Designer: Timothy Meaker

All That Trouble That We Had

By Paul Lucas

Thu 13 May - Sat 5 Jun

'We're only good people gone slightly desperate'

When you're in despair no action seems too extreme. On one side of a bridge a daughter employs reckless measures to secure the return of her dead mother. On the other side a man reads *Heroes of Crime* and contemplates the craziest of schemes. And always in the background the distant sound of bodies splashing down from the bridge into the river.

But what part does the cheery, cigar smoking postmistress play? And who is the overweight salesman suddenly dropped into their lives? And are these bizarre happenings really chance, malice or destiny?

All That Trouble That We Had is a darkly comic and vivacious tale of wickedness on the margins of society celebrates the hopeless, the lonely and the unsuccessful, and explores our capricious ability to survive in vicious times.

Director: Anthony Clark

After Dark: 6 Jun
(After the perf)

In the Main House

No Such Thing...

Theatre in the 80's
Sat 13 Mar

Michael Billington, theatre critic for The Guardian, celebrates the ground-breaking theatre of the 1980's, joined by leading practitioners for a lively afternoon of show extracts and debate. This landmark event, which will include audience discussion, is the Birmingham Rep's contribution to the Towards the Millennium Festival of the 80's.

Performance: 2pm
Tickets: £5.00
Concs: £3.00

Edited by Merlin Holland
Performed by Corin Redgrave
Music Composed by Jonathan Goldstein

Paddy Irishman, Paddy Englishman and Paddy ...?

By Declan Croghan

CAST

Sean Connolly Peter

Tom Farrelly Anto

Michael Colgan Kevin

Annie Farr Una

Director Anthony Clark

Designer Patrick Connellan

Lighting Designer Tim Mitchell

Sound Dean Whiskens

Fight Director Malcolm Ranson

Stage Manager Niki Ewen

Deputy Stage Manager Ruth Morgan

Assistant Stage Manager Daniel Precious

Production credits

J Sainsburys plc
Del Monte Foods UK Ltd
Avonmore Dairies Ltd
Mike Draper, City Fruits
G. Costa and Co Ltd
Belling Appliances
Cambell Distilleries
Jacobs Bakeries Ltd
United Distillers and Vintners Ltd
Prop. AG. Anda. Ltd

Declan Croghan
Author

Some questions you might ask me about the play.

'Why the title, PADDY IRISHMAN, PADDY ENGLISHMAN, AND PADDY...?' Well... because I wanted it on the top of the agenda and the first line of the story of the play is the title. 'Right...What is a Paddy?' - Eh,...any Irish person living in England will tell you what a Paddy is and so will any English person. However, they will not necessarily give you the same answer. For me, a Paddy is what you are when you have come over first and you are in that transition period of trying to find out who you are, and what you are. You know you are not who you were, or what you were, when you were at home. Also, the personal journey of the young Irish in this play asks the same questions that we are asking as a nation. Casey asked this same question in *The Shadow of a Gunman*. I have taken the framing of that picture he took of his world in his own time; two ordinary lads living together in a flat, a romantic young woman, a gunman, then dipped the lot of it into the soup of Irish/English politics.

The questions are still the same ones: Who are we? Where are we going?

Ten years ago the answers wouldn't have changed much from what they were fifty years ago, or a hundred years ago. But now...? Well, while we have had many false endings to the troubles of our Islands, I don't believe that we have been here before. I don't believe that the maps of the past can be of any use to us in the next millenium.

So, when real peace comes what will that be like? Will we be like the Russians without communism? Will there be anything to sing about, argue about, or write about? Well? Well?... we won't be who we are now, and we will never be who we were again.

So, we take the step through that door and into the future, or do we? I'm not sure that we all will, not the way things are now, and unless we all go through the door then it won't work. It won't work because we will still have more bombs killing people and so we won't be free of it. So we must ask ourselves some old questions. Do we sacrifice the few for the good of the majority? How will we buy that new future without more blood. Those questions are not answered here, but I'd like to think that we have looked at the truth of it. And finally, Why a comedy? Well, why not? To be afraid to laugh at it would really make us all a bunch of cowards. And what ever we are, we're not that.

Declan Croghan worked as a navvy and an actor before becoming a playwright. His plays *Dublin Cowboys* and *Refugees* were both performed at the Eblana theatre in Dublin. *Choirboys*, inspired by his own spells in borstal, was premiered at the Finborough Theatre in London and then revived at the Old Red Lion Theatre also in London in September. Another play, *The Redeemer* was premiered as part of the Cells season at the Finborough in October of this year. He is currently working for United Television writing for *Where The Heart Is* and is also on board for BBC Radio's new writing initiative *Sparks*.

Sean Connolly
Peter

Training: Birmingham School of Speech and Drama

Theatre: Ted Snarget in *Stig of The Dump* (Clarion Productions, National Tour and West End); Bottom in *A Midsummer Night's Dream* (Find The Light Theatre Company); Tony Perrins in *Destiny* (Birmingham Library Theatre Company; leading roles in Stagecoach New Writing Festival (Birmingham Rep and the Swan Theatre, Worcester), Smee in *Peter Pan* at The Midlands Arts Centre; Ade in *Between* at the Belgrade Studio Coventry; Knot in *Good King Wenceslas* (Warwick Arts Centre); Friar Lawrence in *Romeo and Juliet* and Porthos in *The Three Musketeers* for the Redditch Theatre Company; the Boatswain and Adrian in *The Tempest* for Derby Playhouse.
Television: *Relatively Speaking*; the Screen 2 Film *Cruel Train*, *Resnick* (BBC), and *Woof! Bum Note*, *Boon* (Central)
Film: *Jim's Gift*; *The Big Game*
Radio: *Includes Us* (Radio 3); *I Can't Be Ill I'm a Hypochondriac*, *Shades of Black*, *Campion's Ghost* (Radio 4); *A Question of Courage*, *A Little Lower Than The Angels* (Radio 5).

Sean also works as a professional impressionist.

Annie Farr
Una

Born: Enniskillen

For Birmingham Repertory Theatre: Nerissa in *The Merchant of Venice*; Annie in *Dr. Jekyll & Mr Hyde*, Lydia West in *Divine Right*, Foible in *The Way of The World*, and 2nd witch in *Macbeth*, Dame Pliant in *The Alchemist*.
Theatre: Mary Bodle in *The Northern Star* (Fieldday/Tinderbox Theatre Co); Mary in *Juno and the Paycock*, Dorothy in *A Life*, Melda in *After Easter*, and Rachel in

Seasons Greetings (Lyric Theatre, Belfast); Carol in *Stags and Hens*, Sister Mary Hubert in *Nunsense* and Sapphire in *Pinocchio* (Arts Theatre Belfast); *Galloping Buck Jones* and *Get Happy* (Tinderbox Theatre Co); *I Can't Get Started* (Centre Stage); *Man in the Moon* (Virtual Reality); *Antigone* (Pentameters)
TV: *Out of The Deep Pan* (BBC1); *Sus* (ITV)
Radio: *The Clearance of Audley's Town*, *Stranded* (Radio 3); *Now & Then* (BBC); *Dividing Force* (Radio 4); *Feathers*, *A Tall Tale for the Telling* (Independent)
Film: *High Boot Benny* (RTE)

Michael Colgan
Kevin

Born: Keady, Northern Ireland

Trained: Ecole Jacques Lecoq, Paris

First Appearance for Birmingham Repertory Theatre.
Theatre: *Amazing Grace* (Peacock Theatre, Dublin); *How I Learned to Drive* (Donmar Warehouse); the title role in *Ripley Bogle* (Grace Theatre); *Raw Women and Cooked Men* (Warehouse Theatre, Croydon); *Animal Farm* and
The Voyage of the Dawn Treader (Lyric Theatre Belfast); *The Tree Brides* (San Miniato Festival, Italy); *Shakespeare for Breakfast* (Edinburgh Fringe/Singapore Arts Festival)
TV: *Café Society*, *Access Art* (BBC Northern Ireland).
Film: *The Eliminator* (Cousins Pictures)

Tom Farrelly
Anto

Born: Dublin

Trained: Trinity College Dublin & Goldsmiths College, London

First appearance for Birmingham Repertory Theatre.
Theatre: *Early One Morning* (Bolton Octagon); Aidan in *The Wedding* (The Belgrade Theatre, Coventry; Price in *Waiting For Mr. H* (BAC); *Under Milkwood* (Andrews Lane Dublin); Sex, Drugs, Rock and Roll (Beckett Centre, Dublin).
TV: *Father Ted* (Channel 4); *Taking Issue* (BBC); The Clock (RTE).
Radio: *No-One Writes to The Colonel, A Few Crusted Characters* (Radio 4)
Film: Jo Jo in forthcoming feature film *Being Considered*.

Anthony Clark
Director

Since joining Birmingham Repertory Theatre Company in 1990 as an Associate Director, Anthony has directed *The Seagull, Of Mice and Men, Macbeth, Saturday Sunday Monday, Cider With Rosie* (national tour), *The Threepenny Opera, The Pied Piper, My Mother Said I Never Should, The Grapes of Wrath, The Atheist's Tragedy,* (1994 TMA/Martini Award for Best Director), *The Playboy of the Western World, Peter Pan, Pygmalion, The Red Balloon* (1995 TMA /Martini Award for Best Show for Children and Young People), *The Entertainer, Gentlemen Prefer Blondes, Pinocchio, Julius Caesar* and new plays: *Home Truths, True Brit, Rough, Playing By the Rules* (Mentorn First Night Production Award), *Nervous Women* and *Syme* (a co-production with the Royal National Theatre Studio). He also directed both *Confidence* and *Down Red Lane* for the first season in The Door.

Anthony graduated from Manchester University Drama Department (RSC Buzz Goodbody Award '79), spent two years directing at the Orange Tree Theatre, London and a year working with Tara Arts before being appointed Artistic Director of Contact Theatre in Manchester in 1984. At Contact Theatre his wide range of productions included new plays: *Face Value, Two Wheel Tricycle, McAlpine's Fusiliers, Green and Homeland*, classics: *Mother Courage and Her Children, Blood Wedding, A Midsummer Night's Dream, The Duchess of Malfi, To Kill a Mockingbird* (European premiere - Manchester Evening News Best Production Award 87) and *Oedipus Rex*.

His freelance directing credits include: *Dr Faustus* (Young Vic), *To Kill A Mockingbird* (Greenwich Theatre), *The Snowman* (Leicester Haymarket), *The Red Balloon* (Bristol Old Vic), *The Day After Tomorrow, Mother Courage and her Children* and *The Red Balloon* for the Royal National Theatre, and *The Wood Demon* (West End).

As a writer he has had the following plays produced: *Hand it to Them, Wake* and a translation of Tolstoy's *The Power of Darkness* at the Orange Tree Theatre, *Tidemark* at the RSC Thoughtcrimes Festival, *A Matter of Life and Death* at the Royal National Theatre, *Green* and musical adaptations of *The Snowman, The Little Prince* and *The Red Balloon* at Contact Theatre in Manchester and *The Pied Piper* and *Pinocchio* at Birmingham Repertory Theatre.

Patrick Connellan
Designer

For Birmingham Repertory Theatre:
Confidence; *Down Red Lane*; *Rough*;
Pygmalion; *The Atheist's Tragedy*; *Cider
With Rosie*; *The Pied Piper*; *The Grapes of
Wrath*; *Nervous Women* and *Julius Caesar*

Patrick won the Linbury Prize for stage
design in 1987 and has since worked
extensively in the West End and regional
theatre. In 1989 Patrick designed the indoor
production of *Der Fliegende Hollander* for
Bregenzer Festspiele. His most recent
theatre credits include: *Silas Marner*; *She
Stoops To Conquer*; *Leader of the Pack*;
Neville's Island and *The Wedding* (Belgrade
Theatre Coventry); *Misery*; *A Passionate
Woman* (Comedy Theatre); *Salad Days*
(Vaudeville Theatre); *Conduct Unbecoming*;
(National Tour); *Coriolanus*; *When We Are
Married* and *The Rivals* (West Yorkshire
Playhouse); *Misery* (Haymarket Theatre
Leicester); *Macbeth*; *Twelfth Night* and*I
Have Been Here Before* (Mercury Theatre
Colchester); *Time and the Conways*
(Octagon Bolton). Future productions
include *Limestone Cowboy* at The Belgrade
Theatre Coventry and *Top Girls* at Salisbury
Playhouse and The Drum Plymouth.

Tim Mitchell
Lighting Designer

Tim is currently lighting designer in residence
at Birmingham Repertory Theatre where he
has lit many productions, these include:
Hamlet, *Frozen*, *Whisper of Angels Wings*,
The Cherry Orchard, *True Brit*, *Dr Jekyll and
Mr Hyde*, *Romeo and Juliet*, *The Merchant
of Venice*, *Macbeth*, *Old Times*, *Peter Pan*
and *The Atheist's Tragedy* (Gold Medal
Winner at the 1995 Prague Quadrennial)

Other productions include: *The Winter's
Tale*, *Romeo and Juliet* (RSC), *The Red
Balloon* and *The Alchemist* (Royal National
Theatre), *Outside of Heaven*, *Inventing a
New Colour* and *Young Writers Festival*

(Royal Court Theatre), *Someone to Watch
Over Me*, *When We are Married*, *Landslide*,
The Winslow Boy and *The Entertainer* (West
Yorkshire Playhouse) *Dead Funny*,
Wallflowering and *Tess of the D'Urbervilles*
(Salisbury Playhouse), *Song at Sunset* and
the *New Directions Season* (Hampstead
Theatre), *Adam Bede*, *A Passionate
Woman*, *The Importance of Being Earnest*,
Les Liaisons Dangereuses and *Our Boys*
(Derby Playhouse), *A Soldiers Song* (Theatre
Royal Stratford East), *WodeHouse on
Broadway* (BBC TV/Theatre Royal
Plymouth), *As You Like It* and *Anthony and
Cleopatra* (English Shakespeare Company).

Malcolm Ranson
Fight Director

For Birmingham Repertory Theatre: *Dr
Jekyll and Mr Hyde*, *Toad of Toad Hall*,
Peter Pan, *The Atheist's Tragedy*, *Othello*
and *Romeo and Juliet*.
An international career has covered
productions in Norway, Japan, France,
Austira, Germany, Switzerland, Australia
and Broadway.
Other work includes: *Julius Caesar, Faust,
Cyrano de Bergerac* and *The Lion, The
Witch and The Wardrobe* for the RSC; *An
Inspector Calls, The Wind In The Willows*
and *Rosencrantz and Guildernstern are
Dead*, and *Oklahoma!* for The National
Theatre.
West End productions include: *The Scarlet
Pimpernel, Les Liaisons Dangereuses*, and
Peter Pan. He has also directed *Macbeth* at
The Riverside Studios and worked on
Cyrano de Bergerac at Greenwich Theatre.
Television: *Nightingales, Casualty, Howard's
Way, Blackadder* and *By The Sword
Divided*.
Films include: *Edward II* for Derek Jarman,
A Feast of July for Merchant Ivory and
Twelfth Night for Renaissance Films.

The Birmingham RepertoryTheatre Company
Introducing

The Door

Since it was founded in 1913 Birmingham Repertory Theatre Company has been a leading national company. Its programming has introduced a range of new and foreign plays to the British theatre repertoire, and it has been a springboard for many internationally famous actors, designers and directors.

Now the company can present classic, new and discovery plays on a scale appropriate to one of the largest acting spaces in Europe , as well as a consistent programme of new theatre in its studio, by some of the brightest contemporary talent To celebrate this, the space has a new name and a new look.

The Door's programme seeks to find a young and culturally diverse audience for the theatre, through the production of new work in an intimate, flexible space - work, that reflects, defines and enhances their experience of the world while introducing them to the possibilities of

Confidence: Jody Watson as Ella, Robin Pirongs as Ben
Photo: Tristram Kenton

Twins: Imelda Brown
as Mimi and Anne
White as Gigi
Photo: Tristram Kenton

Down Red Lane:
Mathew Wait as Spider
Photo: Tristram Kenton

As the arts in Birmingham have grown in stature, with the opening of Symphony Hall, the achievements of the City of Birmingham Symphony Orchestra and the arrival of the Birmingham Royal Ballet so there has been massive investment in the resident theatre company.

'Birmingham...the workshop of the theatre world."
Michael Billington - The Guardian

New Work at Birmingham Repertory Theatre
- past, present and future

In recent years, Birmingham Repertory Theatre has produced a range of popular, award-winning and critically acclaimed new plays. These include *Divine Right* (1996), Peter Whelan's timely examination of the future of the British monarchy, Debbie Isitt's *Squealing Like a Pig* (1996), Nick Stafford's *The Whisper of Angels' Wings* (1997) and Ayub Khan-Din's *East is East* (1996), a co-production with Tamasha Theatre Company and the Royal Court Theatre, London.

In 1998, Bill Alexander's production of *Frozen* by Bryony Lavery, which starred Anita Dobson, Tom Georgeson and Josie Lawrence, was unaminously praised for its bravery, humanity and humour in exploring the intertwined experiences of a mother, the murderer of her daughter and the psychiatrist who treats him. *Frozen* went on to win the 1998 TMA Barclays Theatre Award for Best New Play.

In the Autumn, thanks to funding from the Arts Council's Stabilisation Scheme, we were able to start programming our former studio space – now renamed The Door – with a year round programme of new work. Opening with the appropriately named *Confidence* by Judy Upton and followed by Maureen Lawrence's *Twins* and Kate Dean's *Down Red Lane*, the theatre aims to provide a challenging, entertaining and diverse season of ten new plays, including two that tour to arts centres and community venues in the West Midlands.

In support of this work the theatre also runs an extensive education and development programme. Two of the

Confidence: Jody Watson as Ella, Robin Pirongs as Ben, Zoot Lynam as Dean.
Photo: Tristram Kenton

plays in this season: Declan Croghan's *Paddy Englishman, Paddy Irishman and Paddy...?* and *Trips* by Sarah Woods started life on the theatre's attachment scheme for writers. Beginning with just an outline or initial idea for a play, the writer works together with other professional practitioners including actors, directors and designers at appropriate stages throughout the writing process, with the ultimate goal a production of the play at this theatre.

Also in the Autumn, the Education and Literary Departments worked together to present *Transmissions*, a project in which young people from across the city of Birmingham, and from the ages of 7 - 25 wrote and presented their own plays with the support of professional playwrights, directors and actors.

If you would like more information on this or other aspects of our work, please contact us on

Tel: 0121 236 6771 x 2108/2109

Ben Payne
Literary Manager

The Birmingham Repertory Theatre gratefully acknowledges the support of the Sir Barry Jackson Trust in its new work development programme

Supported by
THE SIR BARRY JACKSON TRUST

From Page to Stage

An opportunity for students to participate in the process of putting on a season of new plays. Access to the country's most contemporary theatre writers, and a chance to work with directors, actors and qualified teachers in exploring a season of cutting edge theatre - Declan Croghan's **PADDY IRISHMAN, PADDY ENGLISHMAN AND PADDY...?**, **TRIPS** by Sarah Woods and **NIGHTBUS** by Peter Cann.

What's On Offer?

Workshops

On making block bookings, two workshops will be offered. The first involves an exploration of the content of the text; themes and structure etc. to be led by the Rep's Education Department and held at your college. The second will be run by a writer and the Rep's Associate Director Anthony Clark, and will explore ideas behind the writing and the process of producing the piece from page to stage. These second workshops will take place at the theatre.

After Darks

You can choose to come to the shows which are followed by an After Dark (although you are free to choose when you want to come). This is an opportunity to get the performer's perspective first hand, and to capitalise on that immediate response ensuring that your students get the most out of their time at the theatre.

Scripts

Scripts will be published for each play in a programme format. This provides an opportunity for further study of the text's form and content. Each student has their own copy of each play, at the equivalent of just £1.00. (These texts retail at £6.99).

Discounted Tickets

Tickets are available at the equivalent of just £3 per performance. With tickets normally at £9/£7, this represents a huge discount.

Unbeatable Value

Tickets for all three shows, scripts for each student, workshops with directors, writers and teachers and aftershow discussions with the company are included in the price. Stage to Page is a pro-active approach to serve mutual needs. An opportunity to tackle your curriculum in a unique, accessible way. Suitable for students of Culture, Theatre Arts, English etc.

The complete package works out at only £15 (minimum 15 students, no maximum).

What previous participants have said:
'My students don't usually have access to a professional director. It's brilliant'
'This has been the best part of the course for these students...I'm bowled over by the response. Terrific.'
'I really got to understand how complicated it is...I was much more into it because I'd read it...It was great'

For further details or to book please contact Rachel Gartside, Head of Education on 0121 236 6771

Transmissions: young playwrights

Communication, engagement and the start of something new

As Birmingham's only venue dedicated entirely to new writing, The Door is investing in writers of the future. In Autumn 1998 we launched the first part of our project with plays written by 7-25 year olds with staged readings and performances in our new writing house The Door. Short plays were developed in primary schools and through the Rep's young people's playwriting groups, led by professional writers and directors.

Those taking part in **Transmissions** explored writing, speaking, acting and reading their work with the guidance of professionals at every stage in the process. They developed their imaginative and technical skills in creating stories from action, speech and character.

In December the workshops culminated in a festival of performances. Examples of the extracts and scenes we presented include: *Wish you were here* by Modssor Rashid about a man's past returning to haunt him following his release from prison; Adam Godwin's *The Shop* which centred on the conflict of creativity and responsibility; and *Crossroads* by Sharlene Ferguson in which the friendship between two young women is placed on the line following a night on the town and an unexpected revelation. In all we presented twenty-eight pieces of writing over a two week period.

Photos: Alan Wood

There will be further **Transmissions** projects, including the continuation of the Rep's young playwright's group, which is now entering its third year. Many young playwrights from this group have gone on to develop their writing through higher education courses such as Theatre Arts or Drama at University.

'*I learnt a lot about the hard work that is put into writing a play*'
VINETA JAIN, SWANSHURST SCHOOL

'*Helpful encouraging, insightful, inspiring*'
TIM JEFFRIES, YOUNG WRITER

'*Thank you for the chance to work with some inspiring young people*'
MAYA CHOWDHRY, WRITER

'*Young writers were exposed to a lot of talented professionals, inspired and encouraged to work and to believe in themselves. A lot of young people from the local community benefited.*'
(THERSA HESKINS, FREELANCE DIRECTOR).

'*The festival has given me practical tools to write my plays*'
ADAM GODWIN, YOUNG WRITER

**For more information please contact;
Rachel Gartside / Liz Ingrams on
0121 236 6771 ext 2142/2104**

What previous participants have said:

'*Shy children came out of themselves and they all contributed to the script. Children and parents thoroughly enjoyed the whole experience*'
TEACHER

Declan Croghan

Paddy Irishman, Paddy Englishman, and Paddy . . .?

faber and faber

First published in 1999
by Faber and Faber Limited
3 Queen Square, London WC1N 3AU

Typeset by Country Setting, Kingsdown, Kent CT14 8ES
Printed in England by Intype London Ltd

A CIP record for this book
is available from the British Library

ISBN 0-571-20128-8

2 4 6 8 10 9 7 5 3 1

Characters

Anto
A young man in his late twenties
from Dublin's north inner city

Kevin
A young man in his early twenties
from a Kerry village

Una
A young woman in her early twenties
from West Belfast

Peter
A man in his thirties from Monaghan

Time: present

Place: Kilburn, London

Act One

Morning.
 *In the blackout we hear 'The Patriot Game' being
sung by Una.*

'Come all you young Rebels
And list while I sing
For the love of one's country
Is a terrible thing
It banishes fear like
The speed of a flame
And makes us all part of
The patriot game.'

*Lights up. Sunrise through the stage right window,
it lights a large bedsit containing two beds, a kitchen
area, and a couch.*
 *One of the beds is occupied by Kevin and the other
by Anto. On the couch is the visitor, who is fully
dressed.*
 *He rises, looks at his watch, then about his person
for a smoke, but has none. He then goes to Anto's
bed, looks about, picks up one of Anto's shoes, shakes
it out, a cigarette box falls out. He takes the box,
lights up one of the cigarettes from it, then puts the
box in his pocket.*
 *He moves to the window, pulls the curtains back a
bit and looks out, draws on his smoke. He then goes
to the table and takes out the cigarette box from his
pocket, removes the last cigarette and puts it behind
his ear. He tears open the box and writes a note on it,
puts it on the table. He then takes his suitcase and*

shoves it under Anto's bed, and leaves. As he closes the door behind him, an alarm goes off beside Anto's bed.

Anto (*his hand shooting out and hitting the alarm, stopping it. He then begins his whimpering*) Oh, God . . . God in heaven . . . Jesus Mary and Joseph, me head . . . Me poor head. Me stomach . . . I need water. (*Searching blindly under the bed and finding an empty pint glass, tries to get a drop out of it.*) Jesus. Kevin? Kev, are you awake?

Kevin (*from under the covers*) No.

Anto I think I have poisining.

Kevin (*moaning*) Shut up.

Anto No . . . Really, I think I'm dyin here.

Kevin Well, keep it to yourself then.

Anto Jesus . . . Oh, Jesus . . . I swear to God, I think I got a bad pint last night.

Kevin Good.

Anto Get us a pint of water, will you? Please?

Kevin Ask me arse.

Anto Please! I'll make the breakfast . . . when I'm better . . . if I'm ever better again . . . If I pull through it, that is . . . (*feeble*) Please . . .?

Kevin (*sticking his head out*) Two pounds.

Anto What?

Kevin Two pounds, and I'll get you the pint of water.

Anto Two pounds?

Kevin Yeh.

Anto Just to go to the tap and fill up a pint glass with water?

Kevin Yeh.

Anto You have your arse.

Kevin Fine. (*Gets out of the bed and goes to the sink.*)

Anto A pound.

Kevin No.

Anto But sure you're at the bloody sink already.

Kevin No.

Anto A pound is a deal.

Kevin One fifty. (*filling a pint glass of water*)

Anto No.

Kevin Mmmmmm. Cool clear water. (*Drinks it down.*) Ahhhh. Lovely.

Anto Okay. One fifty. Give it over.

Kevin (*filling the glass*) I don't know what you're complaining about. You'd pay at least two fifty for a pint of water from a pub . . .

Anto Yeh. Okay . . .

Kevin . . . and then you wouldn't even be gettin it brought over to you. (*going to him with the water*) Now . . .

    Gives him the water.

Anto Well don't expect a tip. (*drinking*)

Kevin Looks like he's gone then.

Anto Gone?

Kevin Yeh.

Anto (*taking a deep breath*) Jesus. The sides of me gullet are stuck together. (*drinking again*)

Kevin (*going to the table*) Hmmmmm. Left a love letter. (*reading*)

Anto I'll kill that bleedin barman. I swear he's tryin to kill me, the Kerry Bastard.

Kevin Here, listen to this . . . And never mind Kerry.

Anto How come it's always me that ends up gettin the bad pint, huh? You'd think me livin with a Kerry man would help protect me from him, but I think it makes it worse. I think he's envious of me.

Kevin Maybe if you and the rest of your cronies from Dublin would give it some rest every now and again about the bloody Sam Maguire, he might not be trying to poison you all. Now, will you listen?

Anto So you admit that there is a conspiracy amongst Kerry barmen to poison all Dublinmen?

Kevin What?

Anto You admit that much then?

Kevin Yes!

Anto Yes?

Kevin Yes. I admit it. All of us Kerrymen know about it. And it's not just the barmen who are in on it. Every Kerry man, woman and child is part of it. Yes! We're all sworn in at birth to the annihilation of all Dublin people and the return of the Sam Maguire to Kerry forever. There!

Anto I knew it.

Kevin Now will you shut up and listen.

Anto I've heard enough.

Kevin Well you haven't heard about this.

Anto About what?

Kevin About this letter that he left, that's what.

Anto He left a letter?

Kevin Isn't that what I'm telling you?

Anto What does it say?

Kevin Will you listen! 'A Chara . . .'

Anto 'A Chara?' (*distracted*) Where's my . . .

Kevin Yes.

Anto . . . smokes. It says 'A Chara?' (*looking for his smokes*)

Kevin Didn't I just read it?

Anto It's not all in Irish, is it?

Kevin No. Shut up and listen. This is all your fault you know.

Anto What's my fault? (*holding up his trousers, checking the pockets*)

Kevin Listen and find out! 'A Chara, my dear comrades . . .' Well?

Anto What? (*shaking them*)

Kevin 'What?'

Anto Yes. 'Well' what?

Kevin 'Well what . . .' Well, Jesus, you're some tulip, is what.

Anto What are you on about? Did you see me smokes?

Kevin You have none. Listen! Listen and then you will know what I'm on about. 'My dear comrades.' That's you and me, in case you're wondering.

Anto I'm not. I had a twenty box. (*shaking out a shoe*)

Kevin And you flashed them all out, high roller that you are. Listen. 'Thank you for your hospitality. You really got me out of a tight spot last night.' Well! . . . Are you listening to this? Well?

Anto What? (*shaking out the other shoe*) What are you on about? (*looking in it*) Will you read the letter! (*dropping it to the floor. To himself*) I had two saved in a box.

Kevin Read it . . . 'I have gone on a rekki . . .' Jesus, Mary and Joseph. A rekki?

Anto Will you read the bloody thing, man! For God's sake, I'm dyin for a bloody smoke here, and all you can do is flap about the place over a bloody note! (*looking under his pillow*)

Kevin 'I expect to be back later today to pick up my stuff. Chucky . . . are . . . la!' Oh, God!

Anto Will you give it over, for God's sake. He's only messin. He's gone to look for a job, or something. (*poking about under his covers*)

Kevin Or something . . . (*getting his smokes*) Bloody right he is. Look! Will you stop looking for smokes that don't bloody exist? You saved no smokes. You never save smokes for yourself. In fact, in the three years that I have known you, lived with you even, I have never known you to have smokes saved for yourself for in the morning. (*lighting up*) Well?

Anto Yes, you're right, I'm a terrible person. Can I have one of those . . . please.

Kevin (*throws him the smokes*) Mooch.

Anto (*drawing on the smoke with much satisfaction*) Jesus, I thought me lungs were goin to crawl out of me rib cage. (*noticing that Kevin is still thinking*) Come on . . . You don't honestly think that he's . . . do you? Don't be stupid.

Kevin Stupid? I'm stupid now am I?

Anto Yes.

Kevin Well maybe you can tell me, in terms I'll understand now because I'm so stupid, maybe you can tell me what exactly you know about him? Well?

Anto I know that he is one of us.

Kevin One of . . . sorry, did you say 'us'?

Anto Yeh. One of us. A paddy . . .

Kevin A paddy?

Anto A paddy that has just come over on the boat and was looking for a place to stay. That's it.

Kevin I see.

Anto If you can't help one of your own then what are you?

Kevin What am I?

Anto Yes. Then what are 'you'!

Kevin Ha . . . It's 'what is he?' is the question. Remember? What is 'he'?

Anto Well, he's not what you think he is anyway.

Kevin Is he not?

Anto No he's not. I don't know where you got such a stupid idea.

Kevin Well, I'm a stupid person. I'm bound to get stupid ideas.

Anto There you go. Now you have it.

Kevin It's not as if the carry on out of the pair of you last night wouldn't be enough to convince anybody of it. Is it? Even if they weren't mentally deficient. (*building*) I mean, I may be wrong, but even somebody with a limited intelligence quota, like myself, would be forgiven for thinking that you both are! Since when did you become the diehard Republican? God . . . ! (*going into the toilet, leaving the door open, talking out of it*)

Anto Singin a few ballads is against the law now, is it? Ballads?

Kevin There's ballads and then there's ballads.

Anto What do you mean by that?

Kevin The 'Sniper's Promise'?

Anto Yeh . . . It's a ballad.

Kevin A ballad? I think it might be a little more than what they are usually used to hearing drunken paddies singin up and down the High Street.

Anto It's only a song, for jasis sake.

Kevin A song? Where did you learn it?

Anto What?

Kevin Learn it, where did you learn it?

Anto Where I learned it . . . How would I remember something like that?

Kevin I never heard you sing stuff like that before.

Anto Stuff like what?

Kevin Diehard I.R.A. songs!

Anto Diehards? They're bloody Irish songs. You're gettin as bad as the fuckin cops. Any Irish man proud of where he comes from is automatically in the I.R.A.

Kevin Well if the cap fits . . . And that's a pound in the swear box.

Anto How?

Kevin 'Fuckin cops.' A pound!

Anto Ffff . . . Okay! Stupid . . .

Kevin We both agreed. That's another child with a full belly somewhere out there in the world.

Anto Yeh, well . . . if this keeps up I'll be buyin them four-course steak dinners. Anyway! I don't care what they hear the paddies singing in the street. So what? So what if it is an I.R.A. song? I'm not apologising for meself. I'm Irish, I am what I am. We're here, we're eh . . . paddies, get used to it. That's it.

Kevin Paddy pride? When did all of this come about?

Anto All of what?

Kevin This sudden conversion, this coming out (*coming out of the toilet*) into being a fire-breathing Republican? (*flushing it, throwing lighted matches back into it*)

Anto I've always been a Republican.

Kevin It's the first I've heard of it.

Anto Well, there you go. Still waters run deep, and all of that. There's no law against it now, you know.

Kevin Now? Ahhh! So that's it. You wait until the world and his brother has signed up to make peace and then declare yourself.

Anto (*as if quoting*) 'As an Irish Republican I have every right to celebrate my history and my cultural tradition. It is my birthright and . . .

Kevin Hoist the main sail!

Anto I beg your pardon.

Kevin Hoist the main sail.

Anto What do you mean?

Kevin I mean, hoist the main sail and we can make good use of all of that hot air that is coming out of you.

Anto Is that a seagoing saying, or something?

Kevin Yes it is a seagoing saying. I see you coming and I get going. Did you get that down word for word from your man last night.

Anto Do you think I have no mind of me own?

Kevin Oh, you have a mind alright. A mind to get into a certain pair of knickers. That's the mind you have.

Anto You're a Kerry bastard. I have nothing more to say to you.

Kevin And you're a horny Dublin jackeen. Are you telling me that this sudden flush of patriotism has nothing to do with the fact the you were trying to impress the knickers off Miss West Belfast up there. (*Points up to the ceiling. Goes to the sink and washes his hands.*)

Anto You're a mad Culchie bastard if I ever knew one.

Kevin So you weren't trying to impress her?

Anto Lured down from the mountain with raw meat!

Kevin Yes or no?

Anto A mental muckah.

Kevin Yes or no?

Anto No.

Kevin No?

Anto No. I was not trying to get into her knickers. That's just your dirty little bogman mind workin overtime. I shouldn't even be encouraging you by taking you serious. You have a defective mentality, you've admitted as much.

Kevin I'm telling you, I hope you don't get us into trouble.

Anto What trouble?

Kevin I told you, I have a bad feeling about this whole thing, about last night, about the carry on, about her, and about him, especially about him! That's all.

Anto Will you relax. Look, even if he is an I.R.A. man, and I said 'if' he is, sure isn't it all over? Huh? Isn't it all over now?

Kevin And what if he is one of the boys who thinks that it's not over? What about that? What if he is an out and out headbanger on a bombing mission? Did you think about that? (*Slams down the pan on the cooker.*)

Anto Ahhh. Me head.

Kevin We'll both end up with a bullet in the head for our trouble.

Anto I'm havin a brain haemorrhage . . .

Kevin You actin the big fella.

Anto There it goes now. I'm losin vision in me right eye!

Kevin Oh, no . . . Nothing is too much for our Anto to handle, he's the bloody Chief of Staff of the Renegades, the Rebel's Rebel don't you know. 'Over here on active service.' What Peace Agreement? Nod. Nod. Wink. Wink. And she swallowing it all, gullible young fool that she is.

Anto And deaf in the left ear. Deaf! I'm not well.

Kevin And you playing up to it!

Anto Me legs! Me legs!

Kevin Fool! (*Goes back to the kitchen area, and switches on all the knobs on the Baby Belling: two rings and a grill. He also flicks on the kettle.*) We'll be lucky if we're not arrested and put in prison. (*Pulls out a frying pan and slams it on the cooker.*) And for what? Huh?

Anto Not now. Oh, no banging . . .

Kevin (*pulls out another frying pan*) To impress a bit of skirt. (*Slams it on the other ring of the Baby Belling.*) On the scent of the Cookstown sizzle!

Anto Oh God . . . (*moving to the toilet*) You're talkin through your arse. He's no more an I.R.A. man than you are. (*Closes the door.*)

Kevin I hope you're bloody right. You made enough of it either way. (*into the fridge*) The whole bloody pub watching the carry on out of you. (*Takes out a plate of sausages, rashers, black and white pudding.*) And it says something about her if she is only interested in you because she thinks you're a renegade, doesn't it? (*Lashes about eight sausages onto one pan, and then six or seven rashers onto the other one.*) I mean, what does that say about the state of the girl's mind?

Anto (*from inside the loo*) Ohhhhhh, God! God! Heal me, Jesus, please! Place your healing hand upon me.

Kevin I'll tell you what it says, (*taking a big knife to the* *rings of pudding, and chopping off about four slices of each*) it says that she isn't playing with the full deck. And no amount of blasphemy out of you will change your predicament in there.

Anto Aggghhhh.

Kevin And what of your state of mind? (*Throws the pudding onto the pans.*) Well, that's very bloody sad indeed, isn't it? What does it say about you? Well? (*pulling out a bag of mushrooms and tomatoes from under the counter*)

Anto God! Lay your healing hand on me arse, and heal the pain! Agggghhhh.

Kevin That's lovely. I don't know what sort of luck you expect us to have with you coming out with that sort of thing.

Anto Cum bi ah, me lord, cum bi ah!

Kevin Fine, but I'd be worried about any man that feels he has to be inventing a new personality! (*Throws a handful of mushrooms whole into the pan.*) A man that feels that his true self is inadequate in some way. 'Bond! Anto Bond, the killer with the winning smile.' Huh? Jesus . . .

Anto I'm losin me intestines in here! I'll soon be just a skin-bag of bones and guts by the time it's over.

Kevin Do you want some cure? (*Gives both pans a good shake.*) Huh?

Anto Okay, but don't make it too strong. I don't want to blow what's left of me insides out with it.

Kevin I shouldn't even bother doing this. I should let you suffer. (*taking out a number of items from the press and the fridge*) Because you know, the hand of God is at work here. Yes. (*pouring into a pint glass*) Tomato juice . . . This is what he does. He sees some fool making a bigger fool of, not only himself, but of all mankind in general . . . black pepper . . . So, he puts the boot in, pulls you the bad pint. Tabasco sauce . . . You should be left to suffer and learn your lesson . . . A swallow of blue label, and the liver salts. (*It foams up.*)

Anto Never mind the sermon. Will you give it to me!

Kevin Here we go . . . (*taking an egg from the fridge and breaking it into the mixture, then bringing it to the door*) I'll give it to you alright. As the man says, 'It will either cure you or kill you, boy.' Open up.

Anto Give it . . .

The door opens, Anto's hand comes out, takes it in.

Kevin All down in one go now. Get yourself sorted. We've got to earn some spawndooligs today or we're up the swanny.

Listens at the door to see if he can hear Anto's drinking the concoction.

Anto Agghhhhhhh. I told you to go easy on the mixture.

Kevin Get it down you. (*looking at his watch*) It's nearly time. (*going back to the kitchen and starting to wash and shave in the sink, using the hot water from the kettle*)

Anto I'm not goin out today.

Kevin Why not?

Anto How can I the way I am?

Kevin Jesus, you're not that bad. (*Refills the kettle and flicks it on.*)

Anto Sure, we'll get by.

Kevin On what?

Anto Sure, aren't you goin out?

Kevin Me? No. (*shaving*)

Anto No?

Kevin No. I have to get those forms stamped.

Anto What forms? (*coming out of the toilet*)

Kevin The ones that I told you about, remember? The visa forms for the African contract with McAlpine.

Anto I thought you weren't goin to take it.

Kevin I didn't say that I wasn't goin to take it, I said I was thinkin about it. Wash your hands. So, I'm getting the forms stamped just in case I want to go.

Anto Why didn't you tell me that you where thinkin of goin?

Kevin I did.

Anto When? I mean, you told me about the interview, but I thought you didn't get it. You never told me that you got the job.

Kevin I told you. You were probably drunk.

Anto Probably . . . So you got the job then . . . (*shaking his hands dry, getting some bread out of the bread bin and sticking a few slices under the grill*)

Kevin Yeh.

Anto Do you think you'll go? (*scooping out the contents of the rasher pan into the sausage pan*)

Kevin I don't know.

Anto You must have some idea?

Kevin I don't.

Anto Are you sure you know what you are doin? (*then using the empty pan for eggs – about four*)

Kevin What?

Anto Are you sure you really want it?

Kevin Why do you think that I went for the interview?

Anto Well, sometimes people just try things out to see if they could get it, you know, be that thing. They don't really want to do it, they just want to see if they could do it if they wanted to. You know what I mean?

Kevin (*business*) No.

Anto Like, say, I went into a hospital wearing a white coat, and then people just started calling me doctor. You see? That would be the most important thing about being a doctor.

Kevin What? You mean, appearing to be a doctor is the most important part of being a doctor?

Anto Yes.

Kevin More important than actually knowing 'how' to be a doctor?

Anto Yes. But you wouldn't do any operations or anything.

Kevin No . . .

Anto No, you'd just see what it is like to get the . . . the respect. You know, to prove that from the outside you can't tell, can't judge the book, you know?

Kevin Yeh . . .

Anto Yeh. So maybe you don't want to get this job, you just want to know you could have it if you wanted.

Kevin Eh . . . Oh, let me see, standing on the Kilburn High Road every morning to see if I will be picked from the Bullock Pack for a day's donkey work, or, taking the opportunity to work my trade as a sparks in Kenya for two years? God, I don't know, such a hard choice to make. Maybe I am deluding myself. What do you think? (*wiping off his face and grabbing out two plates*)

Anto You'll hate it out there.

Kevin Yeh, right . . . (*spreading out the food onto the two plates*)

Anto The food out there is crap.

Kevin What . . . more crap than this?

Anto It is. They eat insects and all. (*ready with the eggs*)

Kevin Hold it. (*Takes the toast from under the grill and puts it on the plates.*) Now . . .

He puts the eggs on the toast.

Anto I bet you get food poising when you get out there.

Kevin They eat the same as us. Tea . . . (*taking the plates and moving to the table*)

Anto (*pouring the water from the kettle into the teapot*) No. You're wrong there. Sure I was talkin to Baldy Mick about it one night . . .

Kevin Baldy Mick Mulcahy? (*getting the cutlery*)

Anto Yeh. (*coming over with the tea, mugs, milk, and sugar*) He was out there.

Kevin Ha. He was never out there.

Anto He was.

Kevin When?

Anto In the Congo with the Army.

They are both sitting.

Kevin I didn't know that. (*Blesses himself and starts to eat.*)

Anto Well, now you see? That's what you should do, talk to some people and find out about it before you go burnin your bridges. (*Blesses himself and looks at the breakfast.*)

Kevin What bridges?

Anto (*starting on his breakfast*) The bridges back.

Kevin Back?

Anto To this . . .

Kevin This?

Anto This here, our arrangement.

Puts down the fork. They look at each other, at the crossroads of the conversation. Anto decides not to go down that route, and turns his attention back to the breakfast.

I don't know if I'm up to it.

Kevin What . . .? No breakfast . . .? You have to eat a breakfast.

Anto You're right. (*Gets stuck into it.*)

They eat away in silence for a bit, except for the loud eating noises. They cannot go back to the previous topic of discussion. The clock chimes out eight.

Kevin Jesus, the time . . . I'd better get a move on. (*getting up and getting his coat on and stuff*)

Anto Will you leave us a few smokes?

Kevin In me will or now?

Anto Very funny.

Kevin There's a twenty box behind the clock. But don't take a few out and put the box back. I'm givin you a twenty box and I want a twenty box back, right.

Anto Right.

Kevin Right.

Anto There's something I want to ask you about.

Kevin Go on.

Anto No, I mean, it's something serious.

Kevin (*stops his business to listen*) Okay . . . Go on.

Anto I had a weird dream last night.

Kevin A weird dream?

Anto Yeh.

Kevin How weird?

Anto I dreamt that I was pregnant.

Kevin Pregnant?

Anto Yeh.

Kevin That is weird. Was I involved in any way?

Anto No.

Kevin Okay. Go on.

Anto It was a baby boy.

Kevin A boy.

Anto Yeh. What do you think that was about then?

Kevin Havin a baby boy?

Anto Yeh. I could feel him comin out of me and all, and I can still see his face and smell him. It was very real.

Kevin What was it about?

Anto Yeh.

Kevin It must of been that bad pint.

Anto Yeh.

Kevin Or . . .

Anto Or what?

Kevin An omen. You know? A sign, a warning.

Anto A warning about what?

Kevin About bein careful. You know, keep it in your trousers for a while.

Anto Hmmmm. Oh, that reminds me. You owe me a score.

Kevin What?

Anto Don't say you don't remember our bet . . . last night. I have a clear memory of you betting me twenty pounds that I wouldn't pull her.

Kevin But you didn't pull her. Made a fool of yourself trying, yes. But pulled her you most certainly did not, my sad companion.

Anto But I did. I'm on for tonight.

Kevin Tonight?

Anto Yes, I'm invited up for dinner. So there!

Kevin Well . . . (*buttoning up his coat*) I'd rather you than me my friend, you than me, that's all I'll say.

Anto Hah.

Kevin When at first we do deceive . . .

Anto What?

Kevin And are you planning on telling her anything about yourself that isn't a complete lie?

Anto You're only jealous. Can't pull, never could, never will. Go way out of that.

Kevin No . . . You're right. I am jealous, I am. I wish I could find some dim-witted, foolishly romantic, emotionally crippled, homesick young girl and fill her head with fantastic lies in order to . . . Hold on . . .

Anto Here we go. A lesson from the master of disaster.

Kevin Hold on, get my pound . . . (*Holds up the pound.*) in order to 'fuck' her, or am I being too blunt. (*Puts the pound in the jar.*)

Anto Can't pull! Never never could, never never will!

Kevin Maybe I'm wrong then? Maybe you don't want to just use and abuse her . . . Huh? Maybe you want to be different from every other horny little Paddy she has met since coming to London.

Anto Couldn't score in a brothel!

Kevin Anyway, (*putting another pound in the jar*) I'll leave you alone to have that wank you're going to have on the strength of tonight. But think about this, she's someone's daughter, someone's little girl, someone's little pride and joy. Bye now. (*going out the door*)

Anto Bastard! (*throwing a boot after him*)

The room falls silent. Anto lies in his bed. He has a go at masturbating.

Bastard! Swine . . .

Gets out of his bed. He hears Una walking around upstairs. He sits on the side of his bed and looks up.

Una . . .

He goes over to the counter and pours himself a small one, drinks it. He then goes back to his bed, lies on it and gets a vision of her in his head. Begins to slowly masturbate while saying her name.

Una . . . Una, Unaa, Unaaaaa.

A knock at the door. Anto freezes. Another knock.

Una Anto . . . Anto, are you okay?

Anto Una?

Una Anto?

Anto Hold on, Una. Just a minute . . . (*grabbing his jeans and putting them on*) I'll be there now. (*tripping towards the door, veering off to the toilet door and closing it*) One moment. (*sniffs. Grabs a can of body spray and sprays it liberally. Coughs, swiping away the cloud of gas, choking, tears in his eyes.*) Coming now.

Una Are you alright?

Anto Fine. Fine. Coming now.

Flattens down his hair and opens the door. She is dressed in a big jumper which covers her like a dress. It hangs off her shoulder revealing a tattoo of a tricolour. She also wears a pair of big open Docs, and that's all.

Una!

Una Anto! (*She sneezes.*)

Anto Bless you!

Una Wait . . . (*another one*)

Anto Bless you.

Una Thank you.

They both wait for a moment.

Are you alright?

Anto Yes.

Una It's just that I heard a loud moaning and I thought . . . Well, I don't know what I thought.

Anto Moaning?

Una Yes. It sounded painful.

Anto Oh, that. No. I'm fine . . . fine.

Una Right.

There is a bit of a silence.

Una Well?

Anto Sorry?

Una Well, do I get brought in?

Anto Jesus, I'm sorry. Come in. Come in. Sit down. Take off your . . . eh. How are you?

Una I'm fine. Hows about ye then, huh. (*going to the chair, sitting on it, crossing her legs*) How's the head?

Anto Aw . . . Don't talk. You know yourself.

Una Ock. Sure don't I just.

Anto There's nothing wrong is there?

Una Wrong? You mean with me?

Anto Yes. Well, no. I mean in general. Anything at all . . . wrong?

Una No. Not that I know about anyway.

Anto That's good.

Una It's not a bad time is it?

Anto No. No. It's just, you know, you've never dropped in before. So I just thought for a moment, when I saw you wearing just . . . your jumper . . . skirt jumper, you know. Not that there is anything wrong with that. I just thought that there was something wrong, like a fire or something.

Una God, a fire?

Anto Something like that.

Una God, no. I just dropped down . . . like you told me to.

Anto Right.

Una You probably forgot.

Anto No. I remember now. Would you like a cup of tea?

Una I wouldn't say no.

Anto Right then.

Una No Kevin?

Anto No. No, he's gone for the day. Yeh . . .

Una Your visitor is gone as well then?

Anto Yeh.

Una Tarry Flynn, what?

Anto Who?

Una The Monaghan man.

Anto Tarry . . .

Una Tarry Flynn. Patrick Kavanagh? Monaghan? (*Monaghan accent*) 'The stony grey soil . . .'

Anto Ahh! Tarry Flynn. 'The Holy Ghost is in the spuds in the fields!'

Una Now you have it.

Anto Sure wasn't it bet into us.

Una And no harm did it do you.

Anto Not a bit.

Una So he's away then?

Anto Who?

Una The Monaghan man.

Anto He is. (*waiting on the kettle to boil*)

Una Right.

Anto But he'll be back.

Una Right.

Anto I think.

Una Right.

Anto I'm not sure.

Una Right.

Anto Yeh . . . A watched kettle, huh?

Una Yeh.

Anto I was singing.

Una Singing?

Anto The sound you heard. The moaning. It was me, singing.

Una Oh . . . Well, it's bound to get distorted coming up through the floor boards.

Anto Yeh.

Una What was it? . . . The song.

Anto Eh, Raglin Road.

Una Lovely, give it a lash.

Anto Ah . . . No . . .

Una Sure it was no bother to you last night. Come on. One man one song.

Anto (*with a forced casualness sings Raglin Road*) Let's see . . .

> On Raglin Road of an Autumn's day
> I saw her first and knew.
> That her dark hair
> Would weave a snare
> That I would one day rue,
> I saw the danger and I passed,
> Along the enchanted way,
> And I said let grief
> Be a fallen leaf,
> At the ending of the day . . .

Una Say no more. (*joking*) Should I leave now? Huh . . .

Anto Sorry?

Una It's Kavanagh again.

Anto Jesus, you're right.

Una Isn't that strange now.

Anto It is.

Una You'll always come back to the cane.

Anto You will.

Una What's bet in stays in.

Anto It does.

Una God I do often yearn at night for a good caning to put welts on me bum.

Anto is staring.

I'm joking, Anto.

Anto Sure I know that. God . . . Ha . . . (*Pokes the kettle, moves it.*)

Una I hope you're not one of those deviants that like to smack girls on the bum.

Anto God no . . .

Una I know what you Dublin fellas are like. Huh?

Anto Ha. And what about Belfast girls?

Una What about them?

Anto Well . . . You know what they say?

Una No. What?

Anto About them being . . . you know. It's probably not true.

Una You never know. Tell me what it is and I'll tell you if it is true or not.

Anto That they are easy.

Una What?

Anto To get into bed. Like I said, I'm sure it's not true.

Una But of course it's true.

Anto It is.

Una But it's true of all women.

Anto All women?

Una All women are easy to get into bed. But they're not as easy to get into bed as men are. (*She smiles.*)

Anto (*getting the joke, he thinks*) Right. (*Kettle clicks.*) Right!

Una Right!

Anto Sugar?

Una No. I have to watch the figure.

Anto Not at all, you've a lovely . . . eh . . . shape.

Una Not by accident. Every calorie ends up there! (*Slaps her thigh.*)

Anto (*coughing*) Milk?

Una A wee dribble.

Anto A dribble . . .

Una It's bigger than I thought it would be.

Anto Bigger?

Una Hmmm. I'm like a mouse up there in the attic.

Anto Ha . . . True enough.

Una You can probably hear me going about the place.

Anto Yeh.

Una Yeh?

Anto Well, no, not really. I mean, I hear you but I don't be listening. (*bringing over tea*) Here we go now.

Una Lovely. Thanks, Anto.

Anto No bother . . . Una. (*getting away again*) I have biccies somewhere . . .

Una You really put the wind up those fellas last night.

Anto I did? (*looking in the press*)

Una Yes.

Anto Eh, which fellas would that be?

Una The gang of fellas that were hanging around outside of the chipper.

Anto Oh, that's right, yeh.

Una They shut up their slagging quick enough when you shouted over, 'Any more of that and you'll be wearing plastic kneecaps!' Ha . . .

Anto Oh, yeh . . . (*embarrassed*) Found them . . . (*coming back with the fig-rolls*)

Una Their faces . . . Sit down, Anto.

Anto Okay. (*obeying*) I hope I didn't embarrass you.

Una Embarrass me? How would you defending me make me embarrassed?

Anto I suppose.

Una It's good to see someone command a bit of respect on the streets.

Anto (*sipping*) Suppose. Fig-roll?

Una Thanks. There's too many people walking around with their heads bowed to the scumbags.

Anto Yeh.

Una They know not to mess with the Boys.

Anto The Boys?

Una The Rah. It's okay, you told me last night.

Anto I did, didn't I.

Una Yes. But you don't have to worry. I'd die before I'd inform on you, or any volunteer for that matter. I grew up in a Republican home. We had our fair share of 'visitors' coming and going. (*Nods.*) So, you don't have to worry about me.

Anto No . . . You mustn't . . .

Una Don't do that, Anto! Don't change it, and lie to me now to protect me. You took me into your confidence last night, and . . . well, that means something to me, alright? Okay?

Anto Okay.

Una No bullshit. That's how we started out, and that's good. (*lighting up a smoke*) I can't talk bullshit, small talk, do you know what I mean?

Anto Yeh . . .

Una I'm getting very serious, amn't I?

Anto You're grand.

Una It's the tea, I can't handle it.

Anto Ha.

Una Have you anything stronger knocking about?

Anto Hmmmm?

Una Than the tay, man.

Anto Eh, yeh, yeh. (*getting up and pulling a bottle of whiskey from behind the counter*) Jemmy okay?

Una I suppose the best will have to do.

Anto Couldn't agree more with you there. (*coming back with the bottle and a couple of glasses*) Here we go.

Una The water of life. (*holding up the empty glass*)

Anto (*opening the bottle. Pouring*) Thank God for the Duty Free.

Una (*holding up the toast*) To the Duty Free . . .

Anto And bone idle customs officers.

They clink.

Una Slanta. (*And she drinks it all down.*)

Anto Slanta . . . (*Watches her drink out of the corner of his eye. Drinks half then quickly finishes as he sees her do so.*) Ahhh. The stuff.

Una Tis. (*sharp intake of breath through the teeth*) That tastes like more.

Anto It does. (*Pours two more.*)

Una Do you know, if we weren't Irish we'd be alcoholics.

Anto We would.

Una Well, *in vino veritas*. (*holding up the glass*)

Anto We who are about to die, salute you! (*the same*)

They laugh, clink, and drink.

Anto A smoke?

Una I will.

Anto (*giving her a light*) Here you go.

Una Hmmmm. (*holding his hand while taking the light. Looks at him. Lets him go.*) I knew from the first time I saw you, when I moved in up there, I knew we'd get on. I can say that now.

Anto Yeh . . .? You liked me?

Una Of course I did, but it took you three bloody months to say hello.

Anto I didn't think you liked me.

Una What?

Anto Well, when you moved in first, I was goin to say hello, but you gave me a look that nearly cut me in two, so I didn't bother.

Una I never.

Anto You did. Jesus it was a real dirty look.

Una I have no recollection of it. Maybe it was the time of the month.

Anto (*empties his glass, ignores the answer*) Top up?

Una Hold on. (*Empties her glass.*) Make it a bottom up. Anyway, we got on fine last night, didn't we?

Anto (*pours*) We did.

Una And we had a good ould heart to heart.

Anto Yeh.

Una A good honest talk.

Anto Yeh. You know, sometimes, sometimes people talk a lot of bullshit when they are drunk.

Una How do you mean?

Anto I mean, it's not always *in vino veritas*. Sometimes they tell . . . lies . . . they just invent.

Una Of course they do. They invent, they relay their heart's desire. You know, some fella tells a girl that he is an airline pilot. Fine. There's nothing wrong with that. It's sad, sad that he's not an airline pilot. He would probably be a very good pilot if it is his heart's desire. So it's still a truth, in here (*chest*).

Anto You think?

Una Yes. But not up there of course. There is a line. I mean, up there it's a 747 plunging out of the sky with hundreds of people screaming for their lives. But in here, in the safety of a secret desire, it is a truth.

Anto Right.

Una But you are right in one respect, in that people have to get half pissed before they can be honest with each other.

Anto Yeh . . .

Una What's the point? You know? I mean, why do we have to get drunk before we can tell each other what we really think, really feel? Why is that do you think?

Anto I don't know.

Una Fear.

Anto Fear?

Una Fear of revelation, of revealing our true selves. We have become a cautious people, Anto, suspicious of the world, and all the things in it, and . . . of each other, especially of each other. And why?

Anto I don't know.

Una You 'think' you don't know, but you do know.

Anto I do?

Una Yes. We all do. We understand these things about ourselves . . . instinctively. Think back to the first time you came over. Do you remember?

Anto Yeh. I was eh . . .

Una You were vulnerable.

Anto Seventeen. I was seventeen.

Una And?

Anto And yeh . . . I was eh . . . homesick.

Una Of course you were. We all were. We miss the things we left. That emptiness, that's the real baggage of the emigrant. We carry it everywhere. It leaves us 'open'. (*drinks*)

Anto Open . . .?

Una Yeh. We walk into the nearest Irish pub we can find, looking for what? (*She gets up.*) Love? No. Fuck that carry on. No. (*Pours a drink.*) Fuck that . . . (*Drinks.*) No . . . (*Walks, prowls.*) Company? Yes. (*touching things – personal things*) Hmmmm?

Anto Yeh.

Una Yeh . . . Companionship. Company with your own kind. (*looking at a framed photo of his family. Distant*) Our own people . . .

Anto Yeh. (*trying to be light*) The first time . . . When I got here, I headed down to Kilburn, straight off the boat, you know? The back-pack overloaded and the manky old work boots danglin off the back. Yeh. I wouldn't mind but I had a brand new pair of work boots at home, but me Da, he wouldn't let me bring them with me.

Una (*still looking at a picture of Anto's family*) This him?

Anto Yeh, That's all of us. No. He says, 'Are you mad? You don't want to walk onto the site with new boots like that. They'll know you're a green-horn straight away. Here,' he says 'take my old ones.' And then he says, 'Remember to piss on your hands.'

Una To what?

Anto Piss on me hands. It makes the skin on them hard.

Una And did you, do you?

Anto No.

Una Right.

Anto Yeh . . . But anyway. I remember when I got here that I was gettin ready to turn around and go back. I had a return ticket. Me Ma made me buy it just in case I changed me mind. She must of known . . . But I said to meself, 'Right. I'm goin back tomorrow. I'll stay tonight and have a few pints. So I went into the pub . . . The first thing that hit me was the sound of voices. It was like . . . music to me, you know? And straight away the homesickness started to leave me. I went right up to the bar and just dropped the load on the floor. 'Give me a pint,' I ses. And before I finished it, I had a start and a place to stay . . . (*smiling*)

Una And the landlady over charged you and your boss underpaid you. (*She has put back the picture.*)

Anto (*the smile fades*) True. But you learn.

Una Yes, we do. But what do we learn? We learn to mistrust. We learn to sit on our money so we know where it is. And we learn to hide.

Anto Hide?

Una Yes. We learn to hide our vulnerability. And stay safe in the craic. Huh? We stay safe in the craic and the carry on and nobody gets too serious about anything. Until what? What happens at the end of the night?

Anto The usual?

Una The usual. It all fuckin explodes. There's fellas beatin the shite out of each other up and down the street, and everybody is roaring and shouting, but we all know that it's a cover up. We're becoming emotional cripples, and why, Anto? What are we doing to each other? What?

Anto We're . . . We're . . .

Una We're fucking each other. We're fucking each other to bits, that's what we're doing out there. Two years!

Anto Two years?

Una Yes. That's how long I've gone without. I swore I would wait for him, no matter how long it took . . .

Anto Him?

Una Who?

Anto Him.

Una Him?

Anto Him who?

Una Oh, him. Well, he's someone who . . . Well, I can't describe him because I have never met him. But I have a constant premonition that I will meet him, that he exists, that he is out there. (*looking at Anto*) The problem is, that when I meet him I probably won't see him, because he's definitely Irish and so he's definitely going to be hiding. (*looking closer*) However, I make a point of not letting any likely candidates pass without full inspection. And you, Anto . . . (*holding the line, pouring herself a good drink*) are the first likely lad I've found in two years. (*while putting down the bottle. Eyeballing him*) Don't get frightened. (*She turns and walks away, drinking, smoking . . .*)

Anto . . . I'm not . . . (*Pours himself a large one.*)

Una (*she is at the window, looking out, picking tobacco off her lip. The sun is falling on her, she is framed*) It's my pact with myself. And I keep to it because if I didn't the consequences could be . . . well, not good. So no matter how long I have to go without, I never open up . . . without just cause . . .

Looks at Anto again. He is trying to hide over-
eagerness by being cool and drinking.

Men think women don't have needs, that we are sexual
camels or something. I need, yes, but not just in a
physical way. I mean, yes I masturbate, but . . .

Anto chokes on his whiskey.

Una I'm sorry, Anto. Did I shock you?

Anto No . . . No . . . Please . . . Go on.

Una Are you okay? (*coming to him*)

Anto Yeh. It just went down the wrong way.

Una (*in a put-on common Dublin accent*) I hate that!
(*Smiles.*)

Anto (*in kind*) What do you hate?

Una (*same again*) That.

They laugh. Una places her hand on top of Anto's
hand.

I haven't laughed in a long time either. You make me
laugh, Anto.

Anto Yeh, I have that effect alright . . .

Una No. It's a wonderful effect, a healing. You touch
me here. (*her breasts*) Here is where a woman needs to
have a kind man touch her, heal her. Two years . . . it's
a long time.

Anto It is . . .

Una But I won't be preyed upon, Anto. I won't be
'used'. I'm not a commodity item.

Anto No . . .

Una I won't become one of those sad Irish girls. You know the ones. The ones that every bastard in the pub has had. One of those sad, lonely, over-used, dirty girls. You do know them, don't you?

Anto Yes.

Una Why do men do it? Huh?

Anto Do what?

Una Create them. Turn perfectly normal girls into creatures like that?

Anto I don't know.

Una No. You see, Anto, it's different in that way for a woman.

Anto Yeh.

Una Have you ever done it?

Anto Done what?

Una Fucked a woman when she was drunk and crying?

Anto And crying?

Una And crying.

Anto No.

Una Would you?

Anto I . . . No.

Una What if you were in the act, and she started crying then?

Anto I . . .

Una Be honest.

Anto I don't know.

Una Good. Because that's something that you need to know about me.

Anto You cry?

Una Yes.

Anto Why?

Una Absolutly no idea. Call it 'The Honesty of Random Emotion.' With me it's like . . . what? Eh . . . Erotic roulette. Who knows when we spin the chamber what one we will stop on, or in what moment it will fire? Does that disturb you, Anto? (*pouring herself another*)

Anto No. (*holding out his glass; a gesture of his defiance/ bravery to go the distance here*) I will, thanks.

Una (*smiles and pours him one*) Good. Now we're going to start being honest with each other, Anto.

Anto Okay.

Una And so we have to construct a raft.

Anto A raft?

Una Yes. A place of safety for us both. If we are going to enter into unkown waters with each other, we at least need to have a minimum amount of trust. I mean, I have this very strong feeling about you, Anto. Very, very strong. You trusted me with something very important last night. A piece of information that could get you killed. That's a lot of openness . . . It's the biggest turn-on there is, someone to trust you with their life like that. It touches me deeply, Anto. Something happened, okay. I'm saying it. There, it's out. I'm deeply touched by you . . . In here . . . (*her breast*) Do you know what I'm saying, Anto. In here.

Anto (*mesmerized*) Yes.

Una This is where you are now. In here. That's the way that I am with you. You opened up and let me in. Now . . . now I want to 'open up' and let you in. Yeh?

Anto Open up . . . Let me in . . . yeh.

Una Something has happend here, Anto. Something eventful, a happening. We met and something came alive. What? The embers of a dormant childhood emotion being fanned back to life? Maybe. A newly created unknown star forged out from a synaptic electrical storm? It's possible. A chemistry? Who knows? I don't. Do you?

Anto Do you mean . . . like . . . sort of . . . eh . . . love?

Una Do I? Do I mean 'Love', do I? How do I know what I mean?

She picks up a knife that is on the table from the break-fast. She looks at it, projecting her thoughts into it.

I know what I feel, but I do not understand it, I don't command it, it overwhelms me, I become it, and that is all.

She looks directly into Anto's eyes.

It leads me, Anto. It compels me to . . . what? Can I trust it, now that I am a grown-up, or should I fight it? (*She looks back to the knife.*) I've been possessed by it before. I went hand-in-hand down that road, his life in mine and mine in his, drunk on the danger and in a state of . . . What? Infatuation? Hormone-induced euphoria? Maybe it has no name, but whatever it was, it was real. No matter how that journey ended, no matter how it turned out, it was honest on its own own terms. It was true of me, of my true condition. So . . . What's true of you, Anto?

Anto I don't know. I suppose I don't know that much about myself . . . But I think . . . well . . . I'm . . .

Una Getting there?

Anto Yeh.

Una I think you're getting there too. Do something for me, Anto. Make a contribution to our little raft of trust here. Do something that will make you . . . vulnerable to me. (*Drinks.*)

Anto Em . . . (*thinking*) Something . . . (*drinking/ thinking*)

Una A gesture of good faith. Surrender something to me. You see, Anto, where we are going is a dangerous place. Very dangerous! Very naked and very dangerous.

Anto Okay . . . eh . . .

Una Give me something, Anto. Anything at all. Tell me a secret!

Anto Eh . . .

Una Something that you would never want anyone to know about.

Anto I don't . . .

Una I'm walking, Anto, if you can't give me something . . .

Anto (*blurting*) I peeped on me sister one time!

Silence.

Una Details.

Anto What?

Una I need details.

Anto But . . .

Una But nothing. Where and when?

Anto Fuck . . . Well . . . She was older than me by four years . . .

Una And you were?

Anto Twelve . . . no . . . I was thirteen.

Una Right. Go on.

Anto Well. I didn't mean to do it. I was in her bedroom robbin her records, for a lend, I was goin to put them back.

Una Right.

Anto And well, then I heard her comin up the stairs with her fella. So, I jumped into her closet but I couldn't get the door shut all the way. And so I saw them . . . doin it.

Una (*having waited for more*) 'Saw them doin it.' Won't do, Anto. Saw them doing what?

Anto Sex. I saw them havin sex.

Una You saw her naked?

Anto Yes.

Una Her breasts? You saw your sister's naked breasts.

Anto Yes. Everything. I saw the lot.

Una Everything? You could have closed your eyes.

Anto I tried, but I just . . .

Una You were aroused.

Anto I . . .

Una You had an erection.

Anto Yes . . .

Una Did you wank? Now 'think!' before you answer me, Anto. A lie now would jeopardise everything between us. Did you wank?

Anto (*after some thought*) Yes.

Una Don't be ashamed. That was completly natural.

Anto It was?

Una Yes it was. Let me change the situation here. Say you looked out of that door and it was some fucker fuckin your mother?

Anto Fuckin me ma? (*a picture of it in his mind*)

Una Yes. He's raping her.

Anto That's different.

Una He's come to rob your house but decided to rape your mother while he's there.

Anto Jesus . . .

Una Quick. He's there, he's raping her, what do you do?

Anto I'm in the closet, right?

Una Yes! Come on, Anto.

Anto Fuck . . .

Una It's not that hard. It's happening what do you do?

Anto I kill the fucker!

Una Yes. Why?

Anto Why?

Una Yes.

Anto Because . . .

Una No.

Anto No?

Una No. Because there is no thought process here. You saw the thing happen and you had an immediate reaction. Well . . . almost immediate.

Anto I was a bit confused about . . .

Una Don't worry about it. The point is that you got sexually aroused in one and violently aroused in the other. You had no control.

Anto Right . . .

Una (*leaning to him with the bottle*) You see, Anto, it's a very narrow line we walk between wanting to 'kill' someone (*pouring. Eyeballing*) and wanting to 'fuck' them.

Anto Right. (*taking his drink*)

Una (*taking her drink. Contemplating him over her glass*) You still don't get it, do you?

Anto Not really . . . But . . .

Una Look at me. what am I doing now? I'm sitting here and I'm controlling a very strong impulse. I'm keeping myself within socially acceptable boundaries. Why? Whose decision am I making. You see? These laws we make. We make them for ourselves. Thou shalt not kill, because we are all killers. Thou shalt not fuck thy neighbour's wife, because we are all led around by our urge to fuck . . . Huh? That's the basic human condition right there, Anto. Self-preservation and self-reproduction. Everything after that is collective self-delusion. But watch it! Cause at the end of the day we know that if someone tries to deny us, tries to deprive us, take from us, fuck us in some way, then we do unto others, and we do it whatever way we can. We may use different methods but at the end of the day it makes no difference if a bomb is dropped from a five million pound jet or delivered in a secondhand Escort 1.6 Ghia with a big furry dice in the window, it still gets there, we still kill. Do you see what I'm saying now, Anto?

Anto Yes.

Una Good. (*She has made her way to the window, looking out.*) Because we need to be able to see things the same way, you and I, to share a common vision, to be able to look at our time, the time we live in, and see that it's full of lies. To see that truth, honesty and courage have become illnesses, weaknesses that are part of the natural selection process in these 'New Times'. (*Turns to look at him.*) Do you understand that in any way at all, Anto?

Anto Yes.

Una You do?

Anto Yes I do. (*by way of an answer*) Me Granda was a socialist, you know . . .

Una Really. (*waiting for him to muddle his way through*)

Anto I mean, he was a real one. He fought in Spain with the International Brigade, lost a leg and all. But he said to me one day, it was a day that he had one of his big rows with me Da about politics and religion, it came to blows as usual. Me Granda would lose the head, whip off the peg leg and attack me Da with it. It's funny now to look back on it, but at the time it was scary. The thing would kill you if you got a bang of it. Me Ma got it mounted after he died. It's on a brass stand in the hall-way and his medals are all pinned onto it. When people see it for the first time they are a bit taken a back by it, but once they get the story of it then they rub it for luck. That's what they all used to do when he was alive. They would all rub their lotto numbers off the leg for luck. Mad . . . But me Granda said to me that me Da was a true Paddy Englishman when it came to politics. That he would vote for whichever side put butter on his bread, knowing it was comin out of the mouths of others, and then get on his knees looking for penance and make the church rich. But, I'm not like me Da . . . I'm not a Paddy Englishman.

Una No you're not.

Anto But . . .

Una What?

Anto But I'm not like me Granda either . . . I mean, I don't have that . . . the fury . . . that temper that would rage in him. I don't have it. So I don't know, I suppose, I don't know what I am.

Una Well, (*brightening*) you know what you're not, and that's half the battle, huh? (*encouraging him to smile*) Hmmm?

Anto Yeh.

Una And you're honest. (*looking into him*) Aren't you?

Anto Well . . .

Una Well?

Anto I want to be honest with you. (*Looks into her eyes.*) I want to be . . . (*Looks away from her.*) I don't know how to say this . . .

Una Oh, my God . . . I'm sorry . . . I never realised . . . you and Kevin. I never thought. (*getting up*)

Anto No. No . . .

Una I'm sorry. I don't know what I was thinking. (*moving away*)

Anto No. I didn't mean . . .

Una Look! It's okay. Don't . . . Don't pity me! I'm sorry. (*She makes to go.*)

Anto Wait. (*taking her by the arms. Looking into her eyes*) Listen to what I'm trying to say to you, Una.

Una What?

Anto I want to be that man.

Una That man?

Anto Yes!

Una Who?

Anto Him! That man that . . . That man that you want me to be . . .

Una You want to be him?

Anto I want to be him.

Una Then be that man. Become that person. Do it now. Do it . . .

Anto kisses her. She wraps her arms around his neck.

Una (*pulls her head back*) Sing to me Anto, sing to me.

Anto What . . .?

Una Sing . . .

Begins to kiss his neck. Works on him constantly throughout his singing, her emotions building until she is crying, but she does not stop working on him.

Anto
On Grafton Street in November
We tripped lightly along the ledge,
Of a deep ravine where can be seen
The worth of passions pledged
The queen of hearts still making tarts
And I not making hay.
Oh to love too much and by such by such
Is happiness thrown away . . .

(*Breaking from the song but still holding her*) You're crying . . .

Una I know. Ignore it. Sing, Anto. Sing.

Anto
I gave her gift of the mind,
I gave her the secret sign . . .

Una (*opening his shirt, kissing his chest, weeping more*) Don't stop. Sing. Sing!

Anto
That's known to artists who have known
The true sound of sand a stone . . .

She is now on her knees and kissing his stomach, opening his belt.

And . . . work . . . and stint (*voice breaking*) without stint . . . I gave her . . . Fuck!

Una Now Anto! Now!

She pulls him down onto the floor. She cries out.

Now.

She slaps him in the face.

Anto (*stunned*) What?

Una Don't stop.

Hits him again.

Anto (*aggressive*) Right.

He dives at her.

Una Ahhhhhh!

Wraps around him with her legs as tight as she can.

Anto Ahhhhhh! Jesus.

Bites her.

Una Ahhhhhh!

Pulls his head to her by the hair, looks into his face then:

Shhhhhhhh. Shhhhhhh. (*soothing*) It's okay . . .

Kisses him. They embrace, tenderly now.

Take me to bed.

She wraps herself around him. He stands up and walks with her that way to the bed. Once there, they then get on with it. Then loud footsteps running up the stairs. They stop.

Una The police?

Anto What?

A key trying the door.

Kevin Damn! (*banging*) Anto! Anto! Get up quick!

Anto Jesus . . . Kevin! (*going to the door*) Wait! Wait! I'm coming . . .

Kevin (*bursting into the room*) Jesus! . . . (*out of breath*)

Anto What's wrong with you?

Kevin There's after being a . . . (*Sees Una.*) Eh . . . Oh . . . (*sitting down*) Hello Una.

Una Hello Kevin.

Anto What's up?

Kevin Em, Una, Anto and I have to have a private conversation. Do you mind?

Una No. Not at all. I understand. (*getting out of the bed*)

Anto No wait . . .

Kevin No. Anto! We really do have to talk in private.

Una I'll see you later.

Anto Later?

Una Yes. You haven't forgotten have you? I'm making you dinner tonight.

Anto No. Of course I haven't forgotten. Yes, tonight.

Una Okay. (*Kisses him on the cheek.*) See you then. Bye, Kevin.

Kevin Bye . . . Una.

She exits.

Anto This had better be good, very very good.

Kevin I need a drink.

Anto What?

Kevin I said, I need a fucking drink! (*getting it. Lighting a smoke*)

Anto What's going on? What's happened?

Kevin Baldy Mick . . .

Anto Baldy Mick Mulcahy?

Kevin Yes.

Anto What about him?

Kevin He stops me in the street, he's out of breath, he's been runnin . . .

Anto Runnin?

Kevin Shut up. He grabs a holt of me by the collar, hanging out of me, his face blue. I thought he was goin to croak it. 'Get out of town.' He says. 'Start runnin and keep on runnin.' He says.

Anto He what?

Kevin Shut up you Dublin bastard and listen to what's after happening. There has been a big shoot out down in the pub. There was a meeting going on in the back room . . .

Anto What meeting?

Kevin I don't know, he didn't say, it doesn't matter. It was a meeting in the room of the pub and guess who storms into it with a fuckin UZI submachine-gun? Guess, you Dublin bastard!

Anto I don't know you Kerry cunt!

Kevin Your mate from Monaghan! Your mate from fuckin Monaghan . . . (*drinking the whiskey by the neck*) He storms in and wipes out the whole lot of them . . . Can you believe it. (*drinks*)

Anto Was there many killed?

Kevin He said there was bodies everywhere.

Anto Jesus . . . I wonder what . . .

Kevin What?

Anto I wonder what, you know, what . . .

Kevin Wait!

Anto What?

Kevin Wait . . . (*looking about the room*) Where's the . . .

Anto What?

Kevin His things . . .

Anto What.

Kevin Where's the note?

Anto The note?

Kevin The note he left. (*going to the bin*) He said he would be back later to collect . . . (*opening it up*) His things . . . (*looking about*) His . . .

Anto What are you on about? (*Grabs him.*) Will you stop and tell me what you're on about.

Kevin His things! He left them here. Look!

Hands him the note.

That bloody case he had! Remember?

Anto A case?

Kevin Yes, a case. Jesus Christ! Look man. Look around.

Anto I'm lookin. I'm lookin . . . A case . . .

Kevin He said . . .

Anto (*seeing the corner of it sticking out from under his bed, but not moving and not sure if he should move*) I can see it.

Kevin What?

Anto There. Under me fucking bed . . .

Kevin Jesus.

Anto And there I was not ten minutes ago . . .

Kevin (*taking it out*) Out of my way. (*putting it on the table*) Jesus, the weight of the thing.

Anto I had no idea . . .

Kevin We have to get rid of it.

Anto I mean what's . . .

Kevin Get it out . . .

Anto I thought he was just . . .

Kevin Look! We can go through the whys and where-fores later. Later as in when we get that bloody suitcase out of here. Okay?

Anto Okay. Don't . . .

Kevin Don't what?

Anto Lose the head. Don't lose it . . .

Kevin Lose it? Do you have any fucking sense of the gravity of the situation? Huh? And this . . . (*grabbing the note from Anto's hand*) This has got to be worth a few years now.

> *Lighting it with his lighter, he burns it in the sink, turns on water and washes down the ashes.*

Are you listening to me, huh? I said have you any fucking idea of our situation?

Anto . . . Yes . . . That's a pound . . .

Kevin Shut up! Do you understand that we have aided and abetted a gunman to carry out a murder on God knows how many people.

Anto But we didn't know . . .

Kevin No. We didn't want to know! That's the whole bloody point. Do you not see, that we were supposed to know. It was our responsibilty to know. Ignorance is not a defence for what we have done, for our . . . for our . . . our . . . Fuck! Fuck! Don't just sit there with your mouth hanging open on you like you have no idea what I'm talking about. (*grabbing him by the shoulders*) You stupid stupid Dublin bastard. I knew you would do something like this to me one day!

Anto Get off me you Kerry cunt! Get off.

> *Pushes him away. They lock and roll on the floor.*

Kevin You stupid Dublin fucker!

Anto If you don't stop I'll have to hit you.

Kevin Bastard!

Anto I warned you.

Hits Kevin a good box in the nose.

Kevin Aghhhhh! (*covering his face and stumbling about the place blind*)

Anto Watch where you're . . .

Kevin Jesus . . . (*Trips over the table, knocking it over and sending the case to the floor.*)

Anto (*covering his head, expecting an explosion*) Will you watch what you're doing!

Kevin (*getting to his feet and looking at the blood from his nose on his hands*) Look at me! What am I saying? What am I doing here?

Anto Mind the case!

Kevin Mind what case? What case? This one? (*Kicks it.*)

Anto Don't! (*hiding*)

Kevin This one here! (*Kicks it.*) Why? Do you think that there might be something dodgy in it? Huh? (*Kicks it.*) Something dodgy and explosive, do you think that now?

Anto We can get rid of it! Get it out of here!

Kevin Ha! Ha! Ha! Get rid of it?

Anto Yeh.

Kevin We can't bloody get rid of it!

Anto Why not?

Kevin Because we can't! What the hell do you think we are going to do with it? Throw it out the window?

Anto But . . .

Kevin But! But! But we don't know what is in it, do we? It's locked! It could be just his memoirs. 'The Diary of a Gunman, and Postcards from the Bogside.' Or maybe it's something a lot less boring. Maybe it is something that presents no argument, no reason, no regard for its delivery be it by land, sea, or air, no discrimination. Maybe it is the blind and just indiscriminate bomb within whose fury we are all cut down in true equality regardles of race, creed, colour, or class!

Anto So you think it's a bomb?

Kevin What do you bloody think?

Anto I don't bloody know!

Kevin Do you know anything?

Anto We can . . . We can . . .

Kevin What?

Anto We . . .

Kevin What? We can what?

Anto Leave it somewhere . . .

Kevin Oh, great bloody idea. 'We can leave it some-where.' Why didn't I think of that sooner? Huh?

Anto Yeh . . .

Kevin Maybe we could just take a walk down bloody Finsbury Park and leave it there, beside a bench . . . or no, better still, beside the playground! Some of those little brats are bound to grow up and join the Army, huh? Get them nice and early, brilliant idea.

Anto No. I meant, we can leave it somewhere obvious, suspicous, where people will find it, but we will phone up and tell the police where we have left it.

Kevin Oh, you mean like, we will plant the bomb and then we will phone up and give them a warning.

Anto Yeh.

Kevin Have you lost your bloody mind? Have you lost it completly? Do you know how long we would get in prison if we got caught? Huh?

Anto We could explain.

Kevin Explain what? That we put up Mister . . . What's his name again?

Anto Eh . . .

Kevin You don't even remember his name, do you?

Anto I do . . . I do . . . It was eh . . . Paddy!

Kevin Paddy?

Anto Yeh.

Kevin Paddy what?

Anto I didn't get his second bloody name, alright!

Kevin Well, what was I worrying about then? Huh?
I mean, there's a water proof defence if I ever heard one. A fella from Ireland named Paddy . . . Wait!

Anto What?

Kevin Is that a car stopping outside?

Anto (*going to the window*) Hold on . . .

Kevin I thought I heard a car stopping . . . I need a . . . (*getting a smoke*) Don't pull the curtains back! What are you doing?

Anto Hold on. Shut up! I'm lookin.

Kevin What is it? Is it a car or not? Is it the C.I.D.?

Anto It's a car, but I don't think it's the police . . .

Kevin Oh, God. It's them!

Anto Who?

Kevin Who? Who do you bloody think, who? His mates, that's who. They've obviously heard that he has fucked it up and gunned down half a pub in the process, and now they are coming to tie up the loose ends.

Anto But that's good!

Kevin Good? Are you . . . We! We are the loose ends, you fool. They're going to come in here and shoot us both in the head . . . Let's just get out of here now. Down the fire escape . . .

Anto No! Hold it. Hold it. It's okay. It's Mister and Missus Wilson.

Kevin Mister and Missus Wilson?

Anto Yeh . . . from 56.

Kevin How the hell could you confuse Mister Wilson and Missus Wilson for hit-men?

Anto I didn't. I never said anything about them. It's you. You're raving like a lunatic there.

Kevin Well, is it any wonder?

Anto Well, it's hardly the way to deal with the situation.

Kevin No. You're right. (*getting a drink*)

Anto Give me one of those too.

Kevin Right . . . (*drinking. Handing one over*) We need to spread out the facts of the situation before us.

61

Anto Right . . .

Kevin The facts.

Anto I mean we don't even know for sure what is in the thing.

Kevin No. But there is a high probability . . .

Anto But not a fact.

Kevin No, it's not a fact.

Anto Then we should clear it out of our way. Clear it out!

Kevin The case.

Anto Yes, and all doubts that surround it.

Kevin You mean open it?

Anto Open it? No . . . I meant, let's just get rid of it. Yes! If we don't know what's in it then we can't be held responsible for it.

Kevin Don't be . . .

Anto Yes. Don't you see that the more we know about it the worse it gets? Let's stop while we are ahead. We don't know what's in it so . . . so . . . I've got it. I have it. I know what we can do! Yes!

Kevin What?

Anto What if someone robs it off us?

Kevin Robs it?

Anto Yes.

Kevin How do you mean?

Anto If someone robs it off us then we are being relieved of all responsibilty to the thing, and we are being relieved in a completly innnocent way. Yeh? Victoria Station!

Kevin Victoria Station?

Anto We go down there with it, we turn our backs on it for two minutes, and hey presto . . . it's gone from our life.

Kevin And what about the robbers?

Anto What about them? They get what's comin to them.

Kevin A bomb?

Anto We don't know that.

Kevin No.

Anto No.

Kevin We'll have to open it.

Anto What?

Kevin Yes. We'll have to open it. It's the only way to know for sure what is in it.

Anto Open it?

Kevin It's either that or . . .

Anto Or what?

Kevin Or we phone the police right now and take what's coming to us.

Anto What's coming to us.

Kevin Yes.

Anto Are you mad?

Kevin Right now? Very much so. So what is it going to be. Open it up or call the police?

Anto . . . Open it.

Kevin Okay. Go for it.

Anto What, me?

Kevin Yes, you. You got us into this, so . . .

Anto If I die, and you live, I want you to know that I blame you for my death . . . (*laying it on the table*) That I curse you from the grave . . . Right. (*jiggling with a knife from the table*) Damn it.

Kevin (*having moved to the furthest part of the room*) Are you there yet?

Anto No I'm not! Damn it! (*Bangs it with his fist.*) Bloody thing! (*Hits it again.*) Why are you here? Why? (*Hits it.*) Why are you happening to me? (*Hits it.*) Open! Open you fucker!

Kevin Stop! Stop! I can't take it any longer. Give it to the bomb squad and take the bloody rap.

Anto No! I'm goin to open the thing!

Kevin Don't . . . (*going over to him*)

Anto Get back! (*holding the case above his head*) Back!

Kevin Okay . . . Okay . . .

> *There is silence for a moment. A floorboard creeks outside the door.*

Listen . . .

Anto What? (*lowering the case*)

Kevin (*whispering*) Shut up . . . listen. (*Points to the door.*)

Anto (*whispering*) What?

Kevin Can you hear that?

Anto What?

Kevin Outside. Outside of the door . . . Someone.

Anto No . . .

A knock on the door.

Kevin Don't answer it . . .

Anto I'm not.

A knock on the door.

Kevin Oh, God in heaven see me now in my hour of need.

Anto And me. I'm sorry about the stuff I was saying earlier.

A knock on the door.

Una (*from outside the door*) Anto . . .

Anto (*with relief*) Una . . . (*going to the door*)

Kevin What does she want now?

Anto I'm going to answer the door and find out amn't I? (*shouting*) Coming now, Una. (*opening the door*)

Una (*entering in a hurry with news*) I've just got off the phone with Jimmy Ryan. He told me to come and warn you.

Kevin Warn us?

Una He's just after being raided . . .

Kevin Raided?

Anto But . . .

Una Will you listen? The police were asking him about you two.

Anto Us?

Kevin I knew this would happen.

Una Anyway. Look, it's not going to be too long until they track you down and raid you.

Kevin Track us down. (*to Anto*) Do you hear that? Track us down. We're 'wanted'.

Anto (*to Kevin*) Shut up. (*to Una*) Raid us?

Una Yes. Is there anything that I can do to help?

Anto Help?

Una Yes. To help.

Kevin Eh . . .

Una Look, it's okay. You know you can trust me.

Anto It's not that.

Kevin No, hold on . . .

Una (*making a line for the case*) Does this belong to him, your visitor?

Anto Yes . . . But . . .

Una They can't find this here.

Kevin No . . . (*wandering away from the action, turning his back to it all*)

Una I'll take it with me.

Anto What?

He looks to Kevin who is now busy getting out a cigarette and staying out of it, thus leaving it to Anto.

Una I'll hide it in my place for you.

Anto You can't.

Kevin lights his smoke and pours himself a drink, looks out of the window.

Una Why not?

Anto Because it's too dangerous.

Una Nothing is too dangerous for the cause.

Anto Una . . . that case . . . it probably contains explosives.

Una I don't care.

Anto You're still willing to take it to your room? You'd do that for me?

Una I'm doing it for my country . . .

Anto Right.

Una And for you, because you are a volunteer, and because there is no line to draw between the cause and us, between you and me . . .

Anto I . . . I . . .

Una Later.

She puts a finger over his lips.

I should get this out of here.

She kisses Anto.

Some know only love in all actions, even war . . . (*She goes to the door, stops, looks back to Anto.*) Brave men die but once . . . (*Looks to Kevin.*) But cowards die a thousand times. Slan . . . (*She goes.*)

Anto walks to the door and closes it. He stands there for a while, looking into the wood for something. Kevin sits down and pours himself a whiskey.

Anto (*quiet*) Slan . . . You were right . . .

Kevin Don't . . . (*drinking*)

Anto She is what you said she was. A young, vulnerable, gullible, homesick, lovesick girl . . .

Kevin Jesus. (*looking about for a fresh bottle*)

Anto But you left out one thing. A brave girl. Brave! And what are we?

Kevin I'm too . . .

Anto (*still looking at the door*) I mean, what have we done here, stooped to?

Kevin Have a drink.

Anto Oh, I will, I will. I will have many drinks. Many many many fucking drinks. (*looking at Kevin*) I've learned something about myself here, do you know that?

Kevin Sit down . . .

Anto I have learned something here.

Kevin Here! (*holding the drink for him to take it*)

Anto (*taking it*) . . . You know, I always thought . . . I always thought that I was a brave person. I mean, I knew I was afraid of things, but I always believed that when push came to shove that I would be brave, that I would rise above it.

Kevin You don't . . .

Anto No . . . Listen. I mean, I always thought that I was . . . you know . . . that I would be one of the two little boys. You know? (*Drinks.*)

Kevin (*pouring more drink*) Here . . .

Anto The two little boys. You know the way he comes and saves his mate on the battlefield. I always loved that bit. But I'm not that boy. (*Drinks.*) I'm the cunt who leaves his mate there to die. (*Drinks.*) Worse . . . I send me sister into battle for me. (*punctuating each stab at himself now with a drink*)

Kevin She wanted to do it.

Anto What does that mean?

Kevin It means what it means for her. She is probably right now, for the first time in her life, feeling a true sense of heroism, of importance, of worth . . .

Anto Well, that is one wonderful moment that neither you nor I will ever feel. Give me that. (*Grabs the bottle, fills his glass.*)

Kevin Don't go to town on it . . . do something stupid.

Anto Don't worry. I don't think any amount of drink would make me go up there and take the case back. No . . . I'm terminal, I'm fucked. (*Drinks.*) Where's the smokes.

Kevin Isn't it better that she takes it than that they find it here, huh?

Anto Or that they find it up there?

Kevin I never thought of that . . . You don't think she'd . . .

Anto What?

Kevin If she is caught, do you think she'll . . .

Anto For fuck's sake, Man! Do you not know? Do you not understand? Is there any hint of being an Irishman left in your body? Any shred of the long line of men and women who shed their blood to continue your line to this fucking point? No she wouldn't. She'd bloody well sooner hang than betray us . . . Ha . . . Yes! She would hang before she would betray us. Us! And what are we? (*Drinks.*) And that's not even her bravery, that's just her

fucking simple honesty . . . Simple like steel . . . (*Drinks*.)
The women of Ireland . . .

Kevin Now you're drunk.

Anto And so?

Kevin And so . . . Don't get fucked up in the head! Not
now. Not if they are going to be coming here and asking
questions. Do you hear me?

Anto What are we?

Kevin Do you hear me? (*grabbing him*) Listen to me,
listen! It's done, okay.

Anto What are we?

Kevin Not now. We can torture ourselves for the rest of
our lives over it, but right now, hold it together. Alright!

Anto (*pushing away from him*) You make me sick. No!
Let me rephrase that, 'we' make me sick. We make me
sick. Look at us. Look!

Kevin Hey, fine. After today, we never have to clap eyes
on each other again. Okay.

Anto Yeh. Because that's it, isn't it. We were never
mates. (*drinking*)

Kevin What?

Anto You and me, we were never mates. You were only
using me . . .

Kevin . . . I don't believe . . .

Anto Yes. All of these years that we have shared our
fuckin lives together, you were . . . biding your time.
I was a convenience!

Kevin Jesus . . . (*turning away, looking out of the
window*)

Anto You fuck off to Africa and leave me on the field to die, and you're right! You're right! I'd do the same. I didn't think that I would do the same, not until now, not until I let a young girl put her life on the line . . . No, before that, I was saying, I wouldn't do it. I wouldn't leave you there, I wouldn't . . . No . . . But now . . .

Kevin There's a car pulling up outside . . .

Anto (*not listening to him*) I think I would. I think no matter how much I pleaded and begged God to make me brave, I would still run.

Kevin Two fellas in suits . . .

Anto Run! And leave you to die! My true condition is one of cowardice!

Kevin Are you listening to me?

Anto Yes! . . . No . . . What?

Kevin I think it's them.

Anto Them?

Kevin I think . . .

Anto Right. Right then. No more cowardice, no more! (*to himself*) Be brave you bastard . . . (*Drinks by the neck.*)

Kevin Anto. Look, I'm going to ask you for one thing, and it's the only thing I'll ever ask you for that means anything.

Anto What?

Kevin Don't . . . don't do anything that will get me . . . get me killed, alright? (*goes to the door, listening*) They're in the front door.

Anto Let them come . . .

Kevin No. Stop that shite. What did I ask you? What?

Anto Don't get you killed . . .

Kevin Yes. (*moving away from the door*) They're coming up the stairs. A pact, okay, (*grabbing him*) we stay alive, okay, a pact.

Anto Yeh, we stay alive.

Kevin Pact. (*holding his hand for a grab*)

Anto Pact. (*Grabs Kevin's hand.*)

> *A knock at the door. The freeze. Another knock. Blackout.*
> *End of Act One.*

Act Two

*After the search. In the blackout we can hear Kevin
throwing up. Lights up. We see Anto standing at the
toilet door. We see that the flat has been wrecked.*

Anto Are you alright?

Kevin Yeh . . . (*coming out, ragged*) I'm fine now.

Anto (*looking about the room*) Bastards . . . they really
wrecked the kip. Look at the state of the place . . .
bastards.

Kevin Yeh . . .

Anto (*beginning to laugh, getting rid of some tension*)
Their faces when you started to stand up to them. 'Don't
point that gun at me.' Ha . . .

Kevin (*also laughing but heading to tears. His nerves are
gone*) I thought . . . I thought they were going to shoot
us both in the head! Ha . . . His eyes . . . bulging . . .

Anto And what about the other fella. Going in at you
with the butt of the machine gun. (*doing the action*)

Kevin Oh, no . . . don't make me laugh. I'll be sick. I'm
not well. Ha . . . (*beginning to break up*)

Anto You should have seen your face!

Kevin (*his body beginning to shake*) You should have
seen yours . . . I thought . . . (*putting his head in his
hands*) I thought we were going to die . . .

Anto Where's the drink? (*getting up for it*)

Kevin A drink, yeh. Jesus, I'm sorry. I never lost it like that before. Look at you, not a bother on you.

Anto Yeh. Two large ones. (*pouring*)

Kevin By the way, thanks.

Anto For what?

Kevin For steppin in for me like that the way you did, you know, stopping me from getting out of control . . . stopping them . . . stopping the whole thing from blowing up out of control, you know. That took guts.

Anto Don't thank me for that. Get that down you. I did it without thinking . . .

Kevin Thanks. (*Drinks.*) Ahhh. No. That took bottle.

Anto (*smiling*) Maybe I was wrong about myself. Huh?

Kevin Wrong?

Anto Yeh. When I said that I was a coward. Maybe I was wrong.

Kevin Maybe.

Anto Yeh. Maybe that was it.

Kevin Was what?

Anto The battlefield. The two little boys! I did it. I hopped in for you! Didn't I?

Kevin You did.

Anto Yeh. I was here, wasn't I?

Kevin (*not really wanting to go down that road again. Looks away from him.*) Yeh . . .

Anto Yeh. I was here, you were there, and then there was (*pointing out the spots*) one, two , three, four, five , six . . . six of them . . .

Kevin Three of them . . .

Anto (*not listening to him*) Yeh. And see if the boss man hadn't of come in when he did there would have been bloodshed. Cause I was ready to go with me instincts then. 'Who are you looking at? You what?' I had him locked in with the eye contact, you know? The Eye of the Tiger. He was frozen on the spot with fear. I could have just, Yah! A killer chop in the neck. And yah! A good kick in the bollix. And then just, get up! Get up! A few more boots for good measure, then I grab the gun off him. (*miming the gun*) Now! How do you like it? Huh? The game has changed now yeh. Right, all of yis on the floor, on the floor. 'You what? You lookin at me? I said, are you lookin at me?'

Kevin Anto . . .

Anto (*gone*) You want a piece of me? Huh? You know who you're messin with? Huh?

Kevin Anto . . .

Anto Weellll. (*miming the cocking of the weapon which has now grown from an UZI to an M60*) Ka-chunk! Say hello to my little friend!

Kevin Anto!!

Anto What?

Kevin Will you stop? Please?

Anto Okay. Sorry. Yeh . . . (*moving about the room like a caged animal, still in the moment*)

Kevin Jesus, will you sit down, you're making me ill moving around like that.

Anto Okay. You just relax. Don't be getting upset. Yeh . . .

Kevin You're away with the fairies, aren't you?

Anto Yeh . . . (*not listening to him*) You know, we could make a ballad about that . . .

Kevin Jesus . . .

Anto Shush . . . you'll put me off. It's coming to me now. Hmmmm Hmmmm. Yeh. 'Now here is a story about Kevin and Anto . . . ' (*to 'Twas down by Christ Church . . .'*)

Kevin (*to himself*) I don't believe this . . .

Anto Two sons of Ireland who were both bold and brave . . .

Kevin Space cadet . . .

Anto They faced the guns straight down barrels, and Anto jumped for his best mate to save. And!

Kevin Anto!

Anto Right. I'll finish it later. (*seeing that Kevin has the shakes again*) What?

Kevin (*who is now shaking*) Jesus . . . the shakes are back . . .

Anto Here. (*with a blanket*) Put this around you.

Kevin Me stomach . . . the guts are burnin out of me.

Anto Look at you. You're shakin like a leaf and sweatin like a pig.

Kevin Me breathin . . .

Anto Come on now, breath in and out. In and out. Nice and deep. There you go. It's all over now. It's over.

Kevin (*holding on to the thought*) Yeh. It is, isn't it. It's all over now.

Anto Yeh.

They both sit in silence for a second letting it settle.

Kevin Anto,

Anto Yeh . . . ?

Kevin What do you really think would have happened if the boss man hadn't arrived in when he did?

Anto How do you mean?

Kevin I mean, really, like in reality.

Anto Reality?

Kevin Yeh. Like when the two of us were on our knees pleading for our lives. What do you think would have happened if the boss man didn't come in?

Anto Don't know . . .

Kevin No . . .

Anto We're not goin to tell anyone that, are we?

Kevin No. No, we're not . . .

Anto Right. (*happy again*) You know what your problem is ?

Kevin Tell us.

Anto You worry too much about things.

Kevin Yeh.

Anto Here, what do you think will happen when the cops find out that Donal Daveron is not your man's real name?

Kevin Who cares? They wanted a name for him and so they got one.

Anto Right . . .

Kevin Take that card the boss man left and get rid of it.

Anto Why?

Kevin Why do you think? When Mister Terminator turns up to collect his case the last thing we need him to see is a card with the police hot-line number on it.

Anto He's not goin to come back for that now.

Kevin Did you not listen to one word that the cops said about him. He's a renegade, he being hunted by not only the cops but the provos. He's desperate, he'll be back. (*to himself*) Jesus, I have to get it together. (*getting up, rubbing his face*)

Anto Are you alright there?

Kevin I'm fine . . .

Anto Right. Here have a drink.

Kevin No. No more drink. I need to clear my head. (*going to the sink, running the water*)

Anto No more drink? Are you sure you're alright?

Kevin Yes, Anto. I'm alright. (*throwing water on his face*)

Anto Fair enough. You won't mind if I have one so. (*Pours himself a drink.*) 'No more drink.' (*Drinks.*)

Kevin (*wiping his face*) What we have to do now is focus our minds on how we are going to get ourselves out of this situation.

Anto Yeh, but I think you're wrong about him. No matter how mad he is he's not goin to come into the house with the police outside. (*going to the window, looking out, expecting to see police cars and so on*) I mean . . . They're gone.

Kevin They're not gone.

Anto They are gone. Look!

Kevin They're still there.

Anto Then where are they?

Kevin They're hiding.

Anto Hiding? Why would they be hiding?

Kevin Why do you think? Jesus, Anto, the whole point is that he doesn't see them. It's a trap!

Anto A trap?

Kevin Yes, and we're the bait.

Anto (*almost to himself*) Fuck . . .

Kevin That's only if we are stupid enough to stay here, which we're not. (*pulling out his back-pack from the heap of things on the floor*) Now I suggest that we don't go out together.

Anto What?

Kevin We can toss to see who goes first.

Anto What do you mean?

Kevin I mean, we have to get out of here, Anto. This is over.

Anto Over.

Kevin We have to leave here and go our separate ways . . .

Anto Right . . .

Kevin Right . . .

Anto Where will you go?

Kevin Africa.

Anto You're goin to take the job so.

Kevin Yeh . . .

Anto Right . . .

Kevin Look, Anto. I just want to say, as far as mates go, you know . . .

Anto Yeh?

Kevin Well . . . you're the best one I ever had.

Anto Really? (*surprised*)

Kevin Yeh, really. I owe you a lot, you know.

Anto No. (*trying to make light of it now*) Go way outa that.

Kevin No. Listen. I don't want you thinkin that this is easy for me. When I came here first I knew nothing, you looked after me. I won't forget that, okay.

They are both now on the verge of tears.

Anto Okay. (*Pours a drink.*)

Kevin (*resumes putting things in his back-pack*) What about you?

Anto What?

Kevin Where will you go.

Anto I'm not.

Kevin What? (*Stops packing.*)

Anto I'm staying.

Kevin Staying?

Anto I can't leave her with all this crap.

Kevin Leave her with what? She knows nothing. They'll know she's innocent, for God's sake!

Anto You know what she'll do, Kevin. She'll clamp up and tell them nothing because she thinks that we are the real thing. Jesus . . . She'll go down for this without thinking twice. No. I have to do this.

Kevin For God's sake!

Anto Look, don't be losin the head. If I go down then I go down. If you want to know the truth . . . I won't really mind bein in a high security prison with the world thinkin that I am in the I.R.A.

Kevin You . . .

Anto I mean, maybe it won't be such a bad thing after all, to be like Daveron, to be the shadow of a gunman. (*Drinks.*)

Kevin Now I know you're joking.

Anto Joking? Not at all. I mean, look around. Look at the way we live. We live like pigs. Worse than that. We live like slave pigs. Slave pigs who live to break their backs under a hod and burn out their livers and minds in the pub. It's like a race to see which curse we will end our miserable existence with first. The curse of slavin or the curse of drinkin. (*Drinks.*)

Kevin But like, we move on, you know? We move up. We get out.

Anto For you, yes. You have your trade. That will always stand to you, will carry you out.

Kevin Oh, for fuck's sake, for fuck's sake, man! Listen to yourself. You're a young man only. You can get yourself into a trade, invest a bit of time in yourself. This is not how it has to be forever. Surely you don't believe that, do you?

Anto Don't I? Look at Baldy Mick, and Josey, and Grumpy Keogh, look at all the oulfellas livin in that pub.

They have nothing in this world except for what they stand up in and a spot at the bar. That's the future.

Kevin Do you think that they would have anything more at home? They're not the like a that by accident. They're that way because they chose it. Because they married themselves to a pint of Guinness instead of a woman. Because they are too bloody greedy to buy a new shirt, or a good meal. But mostly because they are so full of damned bigotry and hatred that they have rotted with it. They will never assimilate because they hate the world outside the pub. Don't expect me to pity those fuckers. I know the two sides of them.

Anto I don't pity them.

Kevin It's proper bloody order that they are left to stew in their own bile. That was never going to be me. I left my home to get away from that. (*Using his anger as fuel for packing, he breaks from the packing at times to make a point and then resumes again and so on.*) You've no bloody idea, let me tell you that much for starters, boy. No bloody idea at all what it's like to live in a small village where the like of them hold the whole place by the throat with their gossip. One word from them about a young-fella or a young-girl and that's that. (*We could almost be watching him packing when he left home.*) Do you know, it only takes a 'Oh your wan is a lively filly right enough.' That's it then. Her name is only dirt from then on. Or a young-fella might not be great at their fuckin GAA, God forgive me, and they'll have him marked. 'Oh do you know what that is now, that's the mother has him ruined with the mollycoddlin, has him gone all funny like.' To hell with the lot of them, they nearly had me hung with their damned talk. But I knew I had to get out, to get out to . . . breathe, (*taking in air*) to grow, to . . . to . . . fucking bloom!

Anto Bloom?

Kevin Yes, to bloom! To become a full human being, reach out, touch the world, live, learn and think freely, have new ideas, my own thoughts for myself. Away from the bloody poisonous generosity of the gossips at full flow feeding on the good reputation of some innocent prey, away from the small minds that look no further than the parish pump for their politics. And the fucking fatalism, especially that, that fucking poetic humbleness. Do you know what I mean?

Anto No . . . But then I'm not from the country, I wouldn't have a clue about any of that, you know?

Kevin Well can you understand this, that I want to be surprised by my life, huh? That I have never been here before and I would like some nice things to happen to me. I mean, if you can't understand that then . . . If you thought that this was . . . this is what I would accept as my life, then . . . (*Stops packing.*) No. You're right. If this was to be it, if I believed that this was it, then I'd be with you. I would. I'd be lining up for that prison cell because then you'd be right. We'd be nothing more than migrant hod-carrying slave pigs, and I would rather be in a prison than be that. But you're wrong. (*Goes to Anto.*) Answer me this question, and answer it to me honestly, why did you leave your home?

Anto Why?

Kevin Yes.

Anto Eh . . . To . . . I don't know.

Kevin There must be a reason.

Anto I don't know it.

Kevin Think. Think!

Anto I am, and don't I know the reason.

Kevin Well you should know.

Anto I don't think there was reason. I mean, I just did it, I just ended up here. That's it. That's all.

Kevin Do you not want to go back?

Anto Yeh, but to go back . . . different, you know? To go back made, plenty of dosh and set up. I did it twice, it was great.

Kevin Went back?

Anto Yeh. The last time, Christmas, you remember?

Kevin I do.

Anto Well, I had the dosh, you know, I flashed it out to me brothers and me sisters, the nieces and the nephews. That's a big thing.

Kevin So you haven't been saving.

Anto I have.

Kevin But you've been blowing it all when you go back home.

Anto Yeh.

Kevin That's . . .

Anto What?

Kevin It's . . .

Anto It's what?

Kevin I don't know.

Anto You don't?

Kevin Sorry.

Anto It's okay.

Kevin But it is something . . . you know? (*Lights a smoke.*) I just don't know what.

Anto Right. (*waiting for something*) Have a go.

Kevin What?

Anto Have a go at it, at solving it.

Kevin I don't know . . .

Anto Have a try.

Kevin I mean, a thing like that, well it's . . .

Anto What?

Kevin Well, it's a very complicated thing, you know?

Anto Yeh.

Kevin It's not something that you want to mess about with too much.

Anto Yeh.

Kevin It's a cultural thing.

Anto Right.

Kevin Working-class ethos thing.

Anto Right. (*waiting*)

Kevin Fuck it! (*looking at Anto, trying to think of an answer for his life*) Come with me.

Anto What?

Kevin Come with me. We'll get the case, leave it here, make the phone call and take our chances. Come on. Come with me to Africa and stop the stupidity.

Anto You want me to?

Kevin Yes, I want you to.

Anto But I thought . . . How . . .

Kevin Never mind how. If you want it you'll find a way. But you have to admit that you want it. You can't be so afraid of not getting a thing that you are afraid to admit to yourself that you want it. Admit that you want to stop trying to buy their respect, that you want to be free of it, that you want to . . . see an elephant in your garden.

Anto An elephant?

Kevin Yes. Or a camel in your kitchen, or a bloody monkey in your bedroom.

Anto (*laughing*) Or a kangaroo! Ha . . .

Kevin (*quietening. Looking out, painting the picture*) Or to sit in silence listening to the sounds of the jungle at dusk and watch an African sunset . . . Admit it . . .

Anto (*quiet*) Okay . . .

Kevin Say it . . . Say, I want to watch an African sunset.

Anto I want to . . . I really want to . . . bloom.

Kevin (*holding out his hand to shake*) Okay.

Anto (*taking his hand*) Fuck.

He grabs Kevin in a bear-hug.

Mates! Huh! Mates!

Kevin Mates.

The door swings open. The visitor is standing there.

Peter I hope I'm not interrupting.

They stare at him, trying to hide their knowlege of him.

Anto You're back!

Peter I am.

Kevin Hello . . .

Peter I would have dropped in earlier but I could see that you had company.

Kevin Yeh . . . Yeh . . .

Anto The bastards . . . So you're eh . . .

Kevin So! . . . You're back!

Peter (*looking about*) 'So!' I am. How come they didn't lift yous?

Anto What?

Peter Why didn't they take yous down to the station?

Kevin They didn't need to. They knew we weren't I.R.A. men. Which brings me to a very funny . . .

Peter But they knew that before they came in here, or didn't they explain that to you?

Anto Yeh. They did. They explained that, (*going to the window, trying not be obvious*) didn't they, Kevin?

Kevin Yeh. They went over all that.

Peter Don't worry, they won't make a move for a few hours yet, (*picking up the card from the table*) wait and see who else turns up to the party.

Anto So you know they're out there then.

Peter Of course.

Kevin And you still came back here . . . I don't understand.

Peter Good. (*looking at the card*) They must have been very pleased with you two. Left their card and all, I see.

Anto We just . . .

Peter Helped them with their inquiries. Gave them my name and, so on.

Anto It wasn't your real name.

Peter Obviously not since you don't fucking know my real name.

Kevin So you know we know then.

Peter What do you know?

Kevin That it was you who did it.

Peter It was me who did what?

Kevin That shot those . . . oulfellas in the pub this morning.

Peter 'Oulfellas?' No, they weren't just oulfellas. You don't mind if I have some of your drink, Anto? (*We begin to see that all is not well with Peter.*)

Anto Work away.

Peter Slanta. (*drinking by the neck*) No. They weren't just oulfellas. They were brass, fuckin Army Council! Ha . . . Yeh. That's very fucked up, isn't it?

Anto Yeh.

Peter Yeh . . . (*Drinks.*) So guess what the plan is now.

Anto Don't know.

Peter You'd never guess it, you know why? Cause there's no fuckin plan any more, no plan. It's great, isn't it? The no plan plan. Ooops! Looks like I'm leaking again. Look. (*Shows his bloody dressing under his coat.*) I'm like a fuckin tea strainer. Poxy little two-twos, peppered me . . . They shot me, yeh . . . The fuckin brass shot me. Bastards . . .

Anto Yeh . . .

Peter And you know why they shot me?

Anto No.

Peter The opposite reason that we shot Michael Collins. So, you see, nothing is new, it merely changes for our time. I disobeyed my orders to cease operations and so I was shot. I'm a soldier, that's my lot. But the least I could do was return the compliment, right.

Anto Yeh . . .

Peter How long do you think I will live, Anto?

Anto Don't know.

Peter Guess. Have a guess.

Anto Not long, I'd say . . .

Peter I'd say you're right. Not long . . . Can I ask you something, as one Irish Republican to another?

Anto Yeh.

Peter Hold on. What about him? He's very quiet, isn't he?

Anto He's just like that.

Peter Is he a Republican?

Anto Yes.

Kevin No.

Peter Aha! You see? He's not. Then, what is he? If he's Irish, but he is not a Republican, what is he? (*Takes out a gun.*) What is he?

Anto He's nothin . . .

Peter No, let him tell me. Sittin there . . . What are you? (*pointing the gun*) What?

Kevin I'm nothin . . . I'm nothin at all.

Anto See, I told you.

Peter No . . . You're something alright, something . . . (*forgetting it*) Anto!

Anto Yes!

Peter Tell me the truth now. What did you vote in the Referendum?

Anto Eh . . .

Peter Don't mind the gun. I'm not goin to shoot you. I've only one bullet left and if I'm goin to shoot anyone, I'll shoot the Free State bastard there.

Anto Thanks.

Peter You're welcome. So what did you vote? Did you vote away our claim to nationhood? Were you one of those fools?

Anto Yes.

Peter For what?

Anto For peace.

Peter For peace? A piece of what? You see that's how they did it! They reduced the ideals of the struggle from 'Independence as a Nation' to a squabble for street corners, reduced it from a war to a dog fight. Replaced the Proclamation with what? A white paper on fuckin socio-economics! Fuckin S.D.L.P. Sticky bastards. The Stickies and the Free Staters! They were the real enemies, rotting us away all the time with the lies, watering us down. 'It's not a fight for freedom, it's a fight for Civil Rights.' What fuckin rights? They got their rights now.
    The right to establish little Irish ghettoes on British soil. Make little Catholic 'No Go' areas. (*at the window*)

They must be havin a good laugh at us now. (*almost to himself*) Well, come on then, Mister MI5, I'll show you how to fuckin die, you S.A.S. bastard. (*to Anto*) Who's that in the red Vauxhall?

Anto That's only Mister and Missus Wilson. They do that . . . They sit in the car and listen to the radio for hours on end.

Peter Weird. Nice car but. Fuel injection.

Kevin, looking up, staring at them.

Anto Sixteen valve engine.

Peter It got car of the month there, didn't it?

Anto Did it?

Peter Yeh.

Anto Sun-roof and all . . .

Kevin Fuck yis . . .

Anto What?

Kevin Fuck yis. Fuck yis. Look. This is all a bit too weird for me, mixing the blood oaths of Padraig Pearse with car tips from Jeremy Clarkson. So if you don't mind, I'll just leave you to it. (*beginning to put stuff in the haversack*) I have this thing called a life that I must be gettin on with. Oh, and by the way, (*to Peter*) just in case I never see you again, fuck you, fuck your war, and fuck your gun.

Anto Fuck . . . Kevin! (*to Peter*) Ignore him. He's havin some sort of mental breakdown.

Peter (*pointing the gun at Kevin's back. We see that he is holding his wounds, dripping on the floor*) Well, I'm well fucked, so that's a given. But I'm afraid you won't be going anywhere right now, Mister Free Stater.

Kevin (*still with his back to him*) Oh, I'm afraid I will be, Mister Dirty Harry.

Anto Kevin! Don't be messin! Ha . . . Dirty . . . (*to Peter*) Don't mind him, Kevin. Stay!

Kevin (*turning on Anto*) You can't be serious. Why should I stay? Because he has a gun? Fuck 'em! Shoot me you bastard!

Anto Kevin, are you gone mad?

Kevin Yes, Anto, I'm gone mad. I'm gone mad like millions of other Irish people who have decided to say fuck it. Fuck it! It's not worth another life. (*to Peter*) Can I ask you a question as a Kerryman to a Monaghan man . . . What the hell gives you the right . . .?

Anto (*jumping in front of him*) Don't shoot him. (*to Kevin*) Shut up you mad bastard!

Kevin Anto! Stay out of this. You, you Monaghan muckah! Am I a legitimate target now in the fucking armed struggle? Am I?

Peter (*to Anto*) You'd want to calm down that Kerry fairy for his own fuckin good.

Kevin My own good? More fuckin advice from a little jockey with a big whip!

Anto Kevin! Kevin!

Kevin (*to Anto*) Get away from me. (*going to Peter. Shouting*) Talk to me. Fucking talk to me! What about my fucking aspirations? Well? What about them?

Peter (*shouting*) They're fucking subordinate to this operation, okay?

Kevin (*turning, throwing his hand up*) I don't believe it. My freedom is subordinate to your fight for my freedom! Do you know the only good thing about Monaghan men?

Anto Kevin . . .

Kevin They're all Cavan men's bastards!

Peter Shut –

Pistol-whips Kevin.

– UP!

Kevin (*from the floor*) That's your fuckin solution then is it?

Peter (*kicks him*) Shut it!

Kevin cries out.

Anto Kevin!

Peter I've enough left in me to give you a good hiding. (*kicking him*) Huh? What about Monaghan now? Here's me with barely a pint a blood left in me and I'm knockin lumps out of you.

Anto Bastard!

Hits him a box, sends him to the floor, jumps on him and gets the gun.

Hands on your head, on your head! Hands on your head! Fuck it . . . (*to Kevin*) Give me a hand.

Kevin What are you doing?

Anto I don't know yet. Let me think.

Peter Yeh. That's a good idea, you think. You think real hard there, friend.

Anto I am thinkin . . . and do you know what I'm thinkin. I'm thinkin, how is all of this happenin to me? Huh? I mean, all I did was help you out. I helped you out. You told me that you were over lookin for a start and I helped you out. You just . . . You just . . .

Peter And you told me that you were a Republican.
I wouldn't of had anything to do with you if I had of
known you meant a bar-stool republican.

Anto Shut up! Shut fuckin up!

Una (*entering with the case*) Fuck! (*Closes the door.
Puts case on table.*)

Anto It's okay, Una. Don't be afraid. I have it under
control.

Una Have you really? What the fuck do you think
you're doing? Huh?

Anto What? You don't understand . . .

Una (*going to Peter*) Give us a look . . . (*looking at his
wounds*) Anto, I would very much appreciate it if you
didn't point that gun in my direction. And close your
mouth, I can feel the draft from here. (*to Peter*) What
went on, then?

Peter They called me in for a meeting , and then they
tried to take me in.

Una Why didn't you tell me that you were goin to meet
with them?

Peter Because I had a feeling that this might happen.
And the last thing that I need on my plate right now is
to have to meet your Frankie and tell him why I got you
killed. None of them tears . . .

Una I'm not. Let me see. (*Peels back his shirt.*) Jesus,
Peter . . . It's not lookin good here.

Peter Who are you tellin? Hey . . . None of that. Here,
will you tell me one thing that I always wanted to know?

Una What?

Peter Do you remember the time you were out on Lough Dergh with Frankie and me. Eight years old you were, and you after crying to come out fishing with us, and poor Frankie, he was more like a daddy to you than a brother. He never could take your tears, never . . . But there was you in the boat and you crying for the sun not to go down . . . And he pops you up on his knee and says, 'What's the tears for, Princess? Why don't you want the Sun to go down?' And I'll never forget you sitting there on his lap, just looking up into his face, and you said nothing for the rest of the evening, you just sat there crying those big pearl drops. And I always wondered . . . Did you know?

Una (*soft*) Don't . . .

Peter That night? Did you know that night that Frankie would be shot by the Brits? Was that it?

Una I don't remember . . .

Peter Not to worry . . .

Una I'll get you an ambulance.

Peter No.

Una But . . .

Peter But no. Listen to me. I'm giving you an order.

Una Right.

Peter Get you down that road. Yes! But before you go, you're goin to prime that for me and leave me with a manual remote. Then you can get Brendan Behan there to give them a little phone call. But listen, once you're away . . . well, stay away. Disappear, it's over . . . Now, get on with it.

Una (*opening the suitcase. She presses some buttons they sound like a phone*) Right, Anto, your wish to

become a twenty-four carat rebel is about to come true.
You have a phone number for your man?

Anto Yeh . . .

Una Well, you're going to come up trumps for him.
(*Tosses Anto a mobile phone.*) You'll phone him and tell
him that your visitor has returned, wounded, and ready
for the picking. Don't look so pained, Anto. All is fair
in love and war as they say. (*going back to Peter with
remote*) It's ready . . . Peter . . . Peter. Ah, Jesus . . . Peter.

She kneels beside him, closes his eyes.

I do remember that day, Peter. I cried to go on Frankie's
fishing trip because I saw him put a rifle in his fishing
case. I was a child, but I wasn't stupid. And as you rowed
across the lough, I sat on the bow and listened to you
and Frankie right all the wrongs done to us. Then in that
moment as the sun began to set I realised the danger.
I understood it all and I stopped being a little girl. So,
yes, yes I knew. And when you dropped me off the boat
to my nana's that night, I knew that Frankie would die.

Kevin Jesus . . .

Anto (*having blessed himself*) Kevin . . .

Kevin He's . . .

Anto Kevin.

Kevin What?

Anto Get your stuff and go.

Kevin Yeh . . . Yeh. Right. (*grabbing his back-pack*)
Right, let's . . . You're . . .

Anto Go on.

Kevin You're not stayin here? Anto?

Anto Look. Kevin . . . I don't know what I'm doin.
Okay? But . . . But I'm not leavin her like this. So, go on.
If you go that will be half the problem solved, alright.

Kevin But she . . .

Anto Look, don't make a big deal out of it. Just go . . .
Do it.

Kevin Okay then.(*Gets his back-pack. Stops at the
door.*) I feel that I should say something but I don't have
anything left to say.

Anto Well, that's a good way for things to be.

Kevin Yeh. See you . . .

Anto Yeh.

*Kevin goes, closes the door behind him. After a
second or two:*

Una Why don't you shoot me, finish it off and leave?

Anto I don't know.

Una Maybe you can't leave.

Anto Maybe.

Una Maybe there's nowhere out there to go.

Anto Maybe.

Una Maybe it's me.

Anto Maybe it is you.

Una I'm flattered.

Anto We don't have to do this you know.

Una I know.

Anto I mean, we could both walk out of here.

Una Could we . . .? You know . . . everything is really fucked up, Anto.

Anto I know. But . . .

Una But?

Anto But before it all went mad . . . earlier today . . .

Una That was a long time ago now.

Anto I know it was, but . . . I have a question.

Una What about?

Anto Did you lie to me about . . . You know . . .

Una Did I?

Anto Did you?

Una You tell me. Did you believe me?

Anto Yes.

Una You see. Today I was telling the truth. Or was I? Maybe you're just a gullible fool. Huh?

Anto Jesus. How can you be so . . . so . . .

Una So hard and cruel maybe. Or such a cold manipulator. Do you think I'm pretty? . . . Well, do you?

Anto You know I do.

Una Well you should have seen me when I was a wee thing of fifteen. I was a sight to behold then. (*almost to herself*) I must have been. I must have been surely.

Anto I'd say so.

Una Would you trust me, walk down a quiet road with me hand in hand?

Anto Yes.

Una Yes . . . Why?

Anto I don't know.

Una Shame . . . I was hoping to find that out before
I left here. Find out what it is about me that made young
men trust me. Made them walk down that road with me.
Young soldiers.

Anto Soldiers.

Una Mmmmm. That was my first act for the cause.
It seemed easier to consider it when I looked at them in
their tanks, but when I saw them in their civies, well . . .
Some of them it would be no problem. By and large
most of them just wanted something to fuck, but I could
never get one of those older ones. They would always
take a look at me, into my eyes, and see something that
would turn them away. Maybe I reminded them of their
daughters back home. No. The ones that came to me
and stuck to me like glue were the babies. Young, homesick, gullible young fools, huh? That first one, with him
it was very hard to keep reminding myself that he was a
Brit. You know . . . when I got him to where I wanted to
bring him and they jumped out to take him, you know
what he said? He said, don't touch her. Don't touch her,
she's nothing to do with this. And they laughed. Then
he knew, but I didn't. I started pleading for his life. I lost
the plot you see.

Anto And they shot him.

Una Yes. But it was clean, and without brutality. One
kind steady shot.

Anto And you were fifteen.

Una And I was fifteen. Fifteen and gifted with the face
of an angel and an appetite for people. You see after that
I was able to completely blank out of my mind what it
was that I was doing. I would actually forget about it.
Forget who I really was. I would really be Mary, or

Kathleen, or Sinead. It was a wonderful escape from being Una. I could be free in them, and I could be completly innocent. And when they looked at me like I was a young sweet naive little Irish girl, I was. Then I was. I would be going along the road with them and I wouldn't have the final act in my mind. Instead I would be day-dreaming about him, and thinking to myself that I loved him. And what our baby would look like if it was half him and half me. And where we might live in Birmingham or Liverpool or wherever he was from. So you see, I never lied to them, because at the time I said it, at that time when he looked at me, I believed it myself, at that time, in that moment, it was the truth. I was in love all those times. I made it happen. I made myself fall in love with them. Then we we would get there and I would just switch that off and shut it out . . . What a little gem I was then. What a little find, the perfect spy. And look at me now. I'm twenty-one and I'm over.

Anto But . . .

Una But no. You see, I am over. Just like poor Peter here.

He smiles at Anto.

Look at you pitying me. Look at you sitting there and thinking that I'm a sad little victim and I could be cured with counselling. Look at you . . .

Anto Look at me . . .

Una You know, Anto, if I didn't know better I'd think that you understood me, I'd think that you could heal me, I'd think . . . here is a man who will look at me the right way every day and one day I'll be free. Huh?

Anto I think so. I think you . . . I think we can get out of this.

Una No . . . You see, there are things that I could never realise to you. Times when I lived three lifetimes in one night . . . with comrades that were so brave . . . so brave that they made up for every coward in Ireland. They made up for men like you, Anto. You see poor Peter here in my arms. Look at my dead comrade. Now do you really think that I would ever be able to walk out that door and betray him, betray him and all of the others that have gone before him, before me, do you?

Anto I don't know, Una, cause I'm not a real rebel. You know what I am? I'm a fuckin eejit. Yeh. I mean, that's why I am still here in this room. Not cause I'm brave or anything, no, cause I'm an eejit.

Una I know that, Anto.

Anto Yeh . . . And I'm also a coward.

Una That's also true.

Anto And so are you. And I understand why you're afraid to walk out that door. Everything you know is over, and all your friends are dead. But like it or not, Una, the war is over, and you've survived it, you might not like that but there is nothin you can do about it. You've been ordered to stop, stop and live.

Una Well . . . I'll need to think about that, Anto. Alone.

Anto Right . . . you do that . . . I'll see yeh . . . Maybe?

Una Yeh. Maybe.

Anto goes out the door, leaving it open behind him. Una goes to the window, looking out, smoking. The lights fade on the stage, only light from the window and the open door. Light fades in the window, she smokes, lights stay in doorway.
    Curtain.